Classic

ORIENTAL DISHES

Classic ORIENTAL DISHES

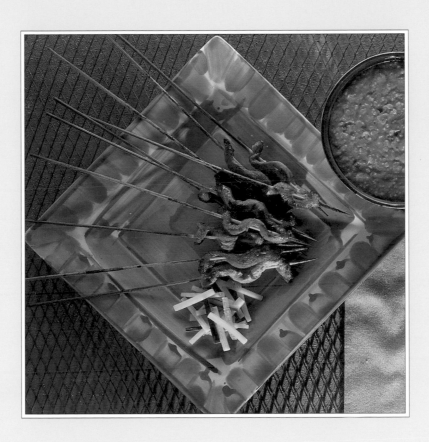

Sue Ashworth • Carol Bowen • Carole Handslip • Kathryn Hawkins
Cara Hobday • Deh-Ta Hsiung • Wendy Lee • Rosemary Wadey

SMITHMARK

This edition published in the USA in 1996 by SMITHMARK Publishers,
a division of U.S. Media Holdings Inc.,
16 East 32nd Street, New York, NY 10016

First published in the UK in 1996

SMITHMARK books are available for bulk purchase for sales promotion and premium
use. For details write or call the manager of special sales, SMITHMARK Publishers,
16 East 32nd Street, New York, NY 10016; (212) 532-6800.

ISBN: 0-7651-9683-2

Produced by Haldane Mason, London

Acknowledgments
Editor: Lisa Dyer
Design: Digital Artworks Partnership Ltd
Photography: Karl Adamson, Sue Atkinson, Iain Bagwell, Martin Brigdale,
Amanda Heywood, Joff Lee, Clive Streeter
Home Economists: Sue Ashworth, Joanna Craig, Jill Eggleton, Carole Handslip,
Kathryn Hawkins, Cara Hobday, Deh-Ta Hsiung, Wendy Lee, Rosemary Wadey

Printed in Italy

Material in this book has previously appeared in *Barbecues, Chinese Cantonese Cooking,
Chinese Szechuan Cooking, Low-Fat Cooking, Quick & Easy Meals, Thai Cooking,
Vegetarian Chinese Cooking, Vegetarian Dinner Parties, Vegetarian Thai Cooking*
and *Wok Cooking.*

Note
Cup measurements in this book are for American cups.
Tablespoons are assumed to be 15ml. Unless otherwise stated, milk is assumed to be
full-fat, eggs are standard size 2 and pepper is freshly ground black pepper.

CONTENTS

INTRODUCTION

The culinary delights of the Orient are explored in this cookbook, bringing together recipes from China, Japan, and South-east Asia. Many of the dishes from these different countries use similar ingredients, and fish and rice are staples. Generally, the food from these regions takes much longer to prepare than to cook, but much of the preparation can be done ahead of time.

China is a vast country, and its food products and climate are similarly varied. Each region has a distinctive style of cooking, from Peking in the north to Canton in the south, and Shanghi in the east to Szechuan in the west, but all emphasize the harmonious blending of color, aroma, flavor, and texture in a single dish or course of dishes. Szechuan food is noted for being hot, spicy, and strongly flavored. Chilies are used in large quantities, and garlic, onions, and scallions are also basic ingredients. Aromatic ground rice and sesame seeds are often used to coat meat, and sesame paste is the principal ingredient in sauces. Beef is the most popular meat, and this region is known for its meat-preservation techniques, such as salting, drying, smoking, and pickling. Yunnan in the deep south-west is an even more remote region than Szechuan and its best-known product is ham, although it is also known for rabbit and venison dishes.

The crispy Peking duck, prepared with hoisin sauce, is the specialty of Peking cuisine, but pork and noodle dishes are also favorites. Standard Cantonese dishes include many recipes that are popular with Westerners, such as egg rolls, egg foo yung, and pork dishes. Fish, shrimp, ground chicken and bean curd are basic ingredients in the cooking of the Shanghai region, and shredded fish and meat are typical of the Fukien region. Although famous for its sushi and sashimi, Japan offers many other culinary pleasures, such as tempura (deep-fried fish or vegetables), sukiyaki and teriyaki dishes, and miso soups.

Indonesia consists of many small islands, and the Chinese, Dutch, and Portuguese have influenced the cuisine of this area. Nasi goreng, a fried rice dish, and gado gado, a salad of vegetables served with a spicy peanut sauce, are served throughout Malaysia and the islands. Thai food is often described as having a greater complexity of flavors and textures than Indonesian or Malay food, although they all rely on the same basic ingredients for cooking. Thailand has a highly unique cuisine that has changed little over the centuries, despite regular foreign intervention. Although the influence of China and India can be seen in the stir-fries and curries, these dishes are adapted by the use of herbs, spices, and coconut milk. The use of galangal, lemon grass, lime, and fish sauce gives Thai food its characteristic flavor.

COOKING METHODS AND EQUIPMENT

*The equipment needed for cooking oriental dishes is easily available to Western cooks.
A wok is useful for more than stir-frying: it can be used for braising, deep-frying, steaming, boiling,
poaching, and even making soups. There are two types available: the traditional iron version and the
modern nonstick version. The traditional wok is extremely reasonable in price, but it must be
"seasoned" first by rubbing oil onto the iron, heating the wok, then rubbing off the excess oil. The
modern version gives perfectly good results and has the advantage of being easier to clean. However,
you will not be able to use metal utensils with these; instead, use wooden spoons, chopsticks, or
spatulas. Many woks are sold complete with these utensils, including a handy rice paddle.
A good all-purpose meat cleaver for slicing, shredding, peeling, crushing, and chopping
is useful, but try out different weights so you find one that suits you. Ladles, spatulas, and chopsticks
are useful for transferring ingredients and stirring. Traditional bamboo steamers that stack on top of
each other are useful, but the wok can be used on its own as a steamer with a rack or trivet inside and
the dome-shaped wok lid on top. It is worth investing in a rice cooker only if you are seriously keen on
oriental foods and eat large quantities of rice. Having said that, most Asian homes have two
or maybe three rice cookers of different sizes and would be lost without one.*

SPECIAL INGREDIENTS

*Many of these ingredients can be found in supermarkets. The more specialist items, such as
fish sauce, black bean sauce, or kaffir lime leaves, can be found in oriental food stores or markets.*

Baby corn Baby corn cobs have a wonderfully sweet fragrance and flavor, and an irresistible texture. They are available both fresh and canned.

Bamboo shoots Still only available canned and sometimes dried (which need soaking before use), bamboo shoots are the crunchy cream-colored shoots of the bamboo plant.

Banana leaves These are the large, green, inedible leaves of the banana tree that are principally used in Malay and Thai cooking for wrapping food and for making containers for steaming purposes. They give the food a slightly aromatic, delicate flavor, but cannot be eaten.

Basil Holy basil, or Thai basil, available from specialist stores, has a stronger, more pungent and sharper flavor than the standard sweet basil. When unavailable, use ordinary basil in the same proportions.

Bean curd Also called tofu, this a food made from blended and pressed soybeans. Sold in flat cakes, it has the texture and consistency of soft cheese. Available plain and bland or smoked, it is highly nutritious and does take on the flavor of the other ingredients it is being cooked with. The type used for stir-frying should be firm so it does not crumble during cooking, and it is best cut into cubes. Don't be tempted to overmix or stir too vigorously during preparation. It is ideal for vegetarian dishes.

Bean sauce A thick sauce made from yellow or black soybeans. The crushed soybeans are mixed with flour, vinegar, spices, and salt to make a spicy, sometimes salty, and definitely aromatic sauce. It is usually sold in cans or jars.

Bean sprouts These tiny, crunchy shoots of mung beans or soybeans are widely available fresh and should be used on the day of purchase. Canned bean sprouts are available, but generally lack flavor and crunchiness.

Black bean sauce Sold in jars or cans, this sauce is made from salted beans that have been crushed and mixed with flour and spices (such as ginger, garlic, or chili) to make a thickish paste. Once opened, keep in the refrigerator.

Chili bean sauce This is fermented bean paste mixed with hot chilies and seasonings. Some sauces are quite mild, but others are very hot. You will have to try out various brands to see which one is to your taste.

Chili paste This is a paste of roast ground chilies mixed with oil. Depending on the chilies used, the color and flavor will differ appreciably, so only add a small amount to err on the side of safety. It is sold in small jars and may be called "ground chilies in oil." A small jar will last a long time if stored in the refrigerator.

Chili sauce A very hot sauce made from chilies, vinegar, sugar, and salt. Usually sold in bottles, the sauce should be used sparingly in cooking or as a dip. Tabasco sauce can be a substitute.

Chilies Fresh chilies come in varying degrees of hotness. Cooking helps to mellow the flavor, but a degree of caution should be exercised when using them. If you do not like your food too hot, then discard the seeds when you prepare the chilies. Remember at all costs to make sure you wash your hands thoroughly after touching them because they contain an irritant that will burn the eyes and mouth on contact. Fresh chopped hot chilies can be replaced with chili paste or powder, but the result will be a little different. As a general guide for buying, the smaller the chili pepper, the hotter it will be. Thai chilies are small and very hot, but the larger types are often stocked in most supermarkets and these are perhaps the best to use when in doubt.

Dried chilies add a good kick to a dish, especially if they are tossed in oil with other spices at the beginning of cooking. Generally, the chilies are added whole, but they can sometimes be halved. In most cases, these should be removed from the dish before serving. Again, the smaller the dried chili pepper, the hotter the flavor.

Chinese cabbage Also known as Chinese leaves, there are two widely available varieties. The most commonly seen one is a pale green color and has a tightly wrapped, elongated head – about two-thirds of the cabbage is stem, which has a crunchy texture. The other variety has a shorter, fatter head with curlier, pale yellow or green leaves, also with white stems.

Cilantro This is a delicate and fragrant herb, also known as fresh coriander or Chinese parsley. The roots have a more intense flavor and are generally used for cooking, while the leaves are used more for flavoring the cooked and finished dish. Chopped leaves are frequently stirred into a cooked dish or scattered over the surface just before serving.

Coconut The coconut is used in many Thai and Malay dishes, both sweet and savory, and is infinitely better to use than shredded coconut. Many supermarkets stock fresh coconuts at little cost.

Coconut milk Coconut milk is an infusion used to flavor and thicken many South-east Asian dishes. Perhaps the best and easiest type to use comes in cans from oriental food stores, but remember to check that it is unsweetened for savory dishes.

Curry leaves Rather like bay leaves, but not quite so thick and luscious, these are highly aromatic leaves that are chopped, torn, or left whole and added to many curries and slow-simmering dishes. Olive-green in color, they can be bought fresh or dried from specialist stores.

Fish paste This thick paste is made from fermented fish or shrimp and salt. It is used only in small amounts since it has enormous flavoring power. Anchovy paste makes a good, if not authentic, alternative.

Fish sauce Known by the name of nam pla or nuoc nam, this salty, thin brown sauce is widely used in South-east Asian cooking instead of salt. It is made by pressing salted fish, and it is available from many oriental food stores. There is really no good substitute, so the sauce is worth hunting for.

Five-spice powder A mixture of star anise, fennel seeds, cloves, cinnamon bark, and Szechuan pepper. It is very pungent, so should be used sparingly. It will keep indefinitely in an airtight container.

Galangal Very similar to ginger, galangal is a root that can be bought fresh from oriental food stores, but it is also available dried and as a powder. The fresh root needs to be peeled before slicing, while dried pieces need to be soaked in water before using and then discarded from the dish before serving. If fresh galangal is unavailable for a recipe, then substitute 1 dried slice or 1 teaspoon of powder for each π-inch piece of fresh.

Ginger Always peel fresh ginger before using, then chop, grate, or blend to a paste to use. Buy it in small quantities to make sure it is fresh, and store it in a plastic bag in the refrigerator. Dried ginger powder is no substitute.

Hoisin sauce Also known as barbecue sauce, this is made from soybeans, sugar, vinegar, salt, garlic, chili, and sesame oil. Sold in cans or jars, it will keep in the refrigerator for several months.

Kaffir lime leaves These are dark green, glossy leaves that have a lemony-lime flavor . They can be bought from special stores, either fresh or dried. Fresh leaves impart the most delicious flavor to a dish, so are worth seeking out. Many Thai recipes call for kaffir lime leaves, and they can be shredded with a pair of scissors or left whole. When stocks cannot be found, substitute a leaf with about 1 teaspoon of finely grated lemon rind.

Lemon grass Also known as citronelle, lemon grass is a tropical grass with a pungent, aromatic lemon flavor. It can be found bottled in supermarkets and fresh in oriental markets. When chopped lemon grass is specified, use the thick bulky end of the scallion-like stem. Alternatively, if the whole stem is required, beat well to bruise so the flavor can be imparted. Stalks keep well in the refrigerator for up to about 2 weeks. When unavailable, use grated lemon rind. Dried lemon grass is also available as a powder called sereh.

Noodles There are many types available, and although some are interchangeable, it is best to use those which a recipe calls for. Choose from rice noodles or sticks, medium–flat rice noodles, rice vermicelli or very thin rice noodles, egg noodles, and "cellophane" or thin transparent noodles. Dried noodles need to be soaked in cold water before using, during which time they double their weight. They then need only a very short cooking time. Fresh noodles do not require precooking and they are cooked in the same way as the presoaked dried variety.

Oyster sauce Oriental oyster sauce, a light sauce made from oysters and soy sauce, is frequently used in Chinese, Japanese, and Thai dishes. It is used to flavor meat and vegetables during cooking. Despite it's name, it is entirely free from the flavor of oysters, or indeed of fish.

Palm sugar This thick, coarse brown sugar has a slightly caramel taste. It is sold in round cakes or in small, round, flat containers. It is not strictly necessary for most recipes and can usually be replaced with dark brown sugar.

Baby corn Baby corn cobs have a wonderfully sweet fragrance and flavor, and an irresistible texture. They are available both fresh and canned.

Bamboo shoots Still only available canned and sometimes dried (which need soaking before use), bamboo shoots are the crunchy cream-colored shoots of the bamboo plant.

Banana leaves These are the large, green, inedible leaves of the banana tree that are principally used in Malay and Thai cooking for wrapping food and for making containers for steaming purposes. They give the food a slightly aromatic, delicate flavor, but cannot be eaten.

Basil Holy basil, or Thai basil, available from specialist stores, has a stronger, more pungent and sharper flavor than the standard sweet basil. When unavailable, use ordinary basil in the same proportions.

Bean curd Also called tofu, this a food made from blended and pressed soybeans. Sold in flat cakes, it has the texture and consistency of soft cheese. Available plain and bland or smoked, it is highly nutritious and does take on the flavor of the other ingredients it is being cooked with. The type used for stir-frying should be firm so it does not crumble during cooking, and it is best cut into cubes. Don't be tempted to overmix or stir too vigorously during preparation. It is ideal for vegetarian dishes.

Bean sauce A thick sauce made from yellow or black soybeans. The crushed soybeans are mixed with flour, vinegar, spices, and salt to make a spicy, sometimes salty, and definitely aromatic sauce. It is usually sold in cans or jars.

Bean sprouts These tiny, crunchy shoots of mung beans or soybeans are widely available fresh and should be used on the day of purchase. Canned bean sprouts are available, but generally lack flavor and crunchiness.

Black bean sauce Sold in jars or cans, this sauce is made from salted beans that have been crushed and mixed with flour and spices (such as ginger, garlic, or chili) to make a thickish paste. Once opened, keep in the refrigerator.

Chili bean sauce This is fermented bean paste mixed with hot chilies and seasonings. Some sauces are quite mild, but others are very hot. You will have to try out various brands to see which one is to your taste.

Chili paste This is a paste of roast ground chilies mixed with oil. Depending on the chilies used, the color and flavor will differ appreciably, so only add a small amount to err on the side of safety. It is sold in small jars and may be called "ground chilies in oil." A small jar will last a long time if stored in the refrigerator.

Chili sauce A very hot sauce made from chilies, vinegar, sugar, and salt. Usually sold in bottles, the sauce should be used sparingly in cooking or as a dip. Tabasco sauce can be a substitute.

Chilies Fresh chilies come in varying degrees of hotness.

Cooking helps to mellow the flavor, but a degree of caution should be exercised when using them. If you do not like your food too hot, then discard the seeds when you prepare the chilies. Remember at all costs to make sure you wash your hands thoroughly after touching them because they contain an irritant that will burn the eyes and mouth on contact. Fresh chopped hot chilies can be replaced with chili paste or powder, but the result will be a little different. As a general guide for buying, the smaller the chili pepper, the hotter it will be. Thai chilies are small and very hot, but the larger types are often stocked in most supermarkets and these are perhaps the best to use when in doubt.

Dried chilies add a good kick to a dish, especially if they are tossed in oil with other spices at the beginning of cooking. Generally, the chilies are added whole, but they can sometimes be halved. In most cases, these should be removed from the dish before serving. Again, the smaller the dried chili pepper, the hotter the flavor.

Chinese cabbage Also known as Chinese leaves, there are two widely available varieties. The most commonly seen one is a pale green color and has a tightly wrapped, elongated head – about two-thirds of the cabbage is stem, which has a crunchy texture. The other variety has a shorter, fatter head with curlier, pale yellow or green leaves, also with white stems.

Cilantro This is a delicate and fragrant herb, also known as fresh coriander or Chinese parsley. The roots have a more intense flavor

Chinese Stock

Makes 10 cups
1½ lb chicken pieces, trimmed and chopped
1½ lb pork spare ribs, trimmed and chopped
15 cups cold water
3–4 pieces fresh ginger, crushed
3–4 scallions, roughly chopped
3–4 tbsp Chinese rice wine or dry sherry

Place the chicken and pork in a large saucepan with the water. Add the ginger and scallions. Bring to a boil and skim the scum off the the top. Reduce the heat and simmer, uncovered, for at least 2–3 hours. Strain the stock, discarding the chicken, pork, ginger, and scallions. Add the rice wine or sherry, return to a boil, and simmer for 2–3 minutes. Refrigerate the stock when cool. It will keep for 4–5 days.

APPETIZERS & SOUPS

A number of dishes can be served as an appetizer before a meal – just like hors-d'oeuvres in the West. Instead of serving different appetizers individually, try serving a small portion of each together as an assorted hors-d'oeuvre, in a similar way to dim sum. Select three or four different items each. Remember not to have more than one of the same type of food, and the recipes should be chosen for their harmony and balance in color, flavor, and texture. Try a selection of Crispy Vegetarian Egg Rolls, Money Bags, and Butterfly Shrimp, for example, or choose a soup to serve as a first course if you prefer. There is a good selection of soups from which to choose on the following pages, from the Thai-Style Chicken & Coconut Soup to Chinese Wonton Soup.

CRISPY SEAWEED

Popular in many Chinese restaurants, this dish is served as a first course before a main meal. This "seaweed" is in fact deep-fried greens.

SERVES 4

INGREDIENTS:
*8 ounces greens
vegetable oil,
    for deep-frying
1½ tsp superfine sugar
1 tsp salt
¼ cup slivered almonds*

1 Wash the greens thoroughly. Trim off the excess tough stalks. Place on paper towels, or a dry dish cloth, and leave to drain.

2 ▲ Using a sharp knife, finely shred the greens and spread them out on paper towels for about 30 minutes to dry.

3 ▲ Heat the oil in a wok or deep-fat fryer. Remove the pan from the heat and add the greens in batches. Return the pan to the heat and deep-fry the greens until they begin to float to the surface of the oil and become translucent and crinkled. Remove the greens, using a perforated spoon, and drain on paper towels. Keep each batch warm.

4 ▼ Mix the sugar and salt together, sprinkle over the "seaweed," and toss together to mix well.

5 ▼ Add the slivered almonds to the hot oil and fry them until lightly golden. Remove with a perforated spoon and drain on paper towels.

6 Serve the crispy "seaweed" with the slivered almonds.

SWEET & SOUR CUCUMBER

Chunks of cucumber are marinated in vinegar and sweetened with honey to make a sweet and sour appetizer.

SERVES 4

INGREDIENTS:
1 cucumber
1 tsp salt
2 tsp honey
2 tbsp rice vinegar
3 tbsp chopped fresh
   cilantro
2 tsp sesame oil
‡ tsp crushed red peppercorns
strips of red and yellow bell pepper,
   to garnish

1 ▼ Peel thin strips off the cucumber along the length. Cut the cucumber in quarters lengthwise, and then into 1-inch long pieces. Place the cucumber in a colander.

2 ▼ Sprinkle the salt over the cucumber and let rest for 30 minutes to allow the salt to draw out the excess water from the cucumber.

3 Rinse the cucumber well to remove the salt and pat dry with paper towels.

4 ▼ Place the cucumber in a bowl. Combine the honey with the vinegar and pour over. Mix together and let marinate for 15 minutes.

5 ▼ Stir the cilantro and sesame oil into the cucumbers, then transfer to a serving bowl.

6 Sprinkle over the crushed red peppercorns. Serve garnishished with strips of red and yellow bell pepper.

CRUDITES WITH SHRIMP SAUCE

This is a classic Thai appetizer – fruit and vegetable crudités served with a spicy, garlicky shrimp sauce. It is served at every meal, and each family has their own favorite recipe. Hard-cooked quails' eggs are a traditional addition to this platter, and you may like to include some.

SERVES 6

INGREDIENTS:
about 1½ pounds prepared raw fruit and vegetables, such as broccoli, cauliflower, apple, pineapple, cucumber, celery, bell peppers, and mushrooms

SHRIMP SAUCE:
2 ounces dried shrimps
½-inch cube shrimp paste
3 garlic cloves, crushed
4 red chilies, deseeded and chopped
6 stems fresh cilantro, coarsely chopped
3 tbsp lime juice
Thai fish sauce, to taste
brown sugar, to taste

1 To make the sauce, first soak the dried shrimps in warm water for 10 minutes.

2 ▼ Then place the shrimp paste, drained soaked shrimps, garlic, chilies, and cilantro in a food processor or blender, and process until well chopped but not smooth.

3 ▲ Transfer the sauce mixture to a bowl and add the lime juice, mixing well.

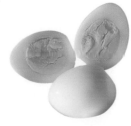

4 ▲ Add fish sauce and brown sugar to the sauce to taste, mixing to blend well. Cover the bowl tightly and chill the sauce in the refrigerator for at least 12 hours, or overnight.

5 To serve, arrange the fruit and vegetables attractively on a large serving plate. Place the prepared sauce in the center for dipping.

CRISPY VEGETARIAN EGG ROLLS

This recipe uses a cornstarch paste. To make the paste, mix 1 part of cornstarch with about 1½ parts cold water, until smooth. For a nonvegetarian version of these egg rolls, just replace mushrooms with chicken or pork, and replace the carrots with shrimp.

MAKES 12 ROLLS

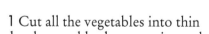

INGREDIENTS:
2 cups fresh bean sprouts, washed and
    drained
2 ounces scallions
2 ounces carrots
2 ounces canned sliced bamboo shoots,
    rinsed and drained
2 ounces mushrooms
2–3 tbsp vegetable oil, plus oil for
    deep-frying
¼ tsp salt
¼ tsp sugar
1 tbsp light soy sauce
1 tsp Chinese rice wine or dry sherry
12 egg roll skins, defrosted if frozen
1 tbsp cornstarch paste
flour, for dusting
vegetable oil, for deep-frying

1 Cut all the vegetables into thin shreds, roughly the same size and shape as the bean sprouts.

2 Heat the oil in a hot wok and stir-fry the vegetables for about 1 minute. Add the salt, sugar, soy sauce, and wine, and continue stirring for 1½–2 minutes. Remove the vegetables from the wok with a perforated spoon and place in a bowl. Drain off the excess liquid, then let cool.

3 ▼ To make the egg rolls, place about 2 tablespoons of the vegetables one-third of the way down on an egg roll skin, with the triangle pointing away from you.

4 ▼ Lift the lower flap over the filling and fold in one end.

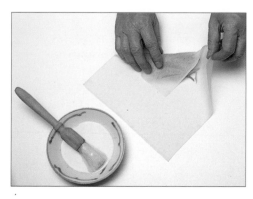

5 ▼ Roll once and fold in the other end.

6 Roll once more, brush the upper edge of the egg roll with a little cornstarch paste, and roll into a neat package. Lightly dust a tray with flour and place the egg roll with the flap-side down. Make the rest of the egg rolls in the same way.

7 Heat the oil in a wok or deep-fryer until smoking, then reduce the heat to low and deep-fry the egg rolls in batches for 2–3 minutes, or until golden and crispy. Remove with a perforated spoon and drain on paper towels. Serve hot with a dipping sauce, such as soy sauce, sweet and sour sauce, or chili sauce.

RICE CUBES WITH DIPPING SAUCE

Plain rice cubes are a good foil to any piquant dipping sauce, and they are often served with satay to complement the dipping sauce. Basmati rice could be substituted for the jasmine rice, but avoid using any rice labeled "easy cook" or "parboiled."

SERVES 4–6

INGREDIENTS:
1½ cups Thai jasmine rice
5 cups water

CILANTRO
DIPPING SAUCE:
1 garlic clove
2 tsp salt
1 tbsp black peppercorns
*1 cup washed and chopped fresh
   cilantro, including roots and stem*
3 tbsp lemon juice
¾ cup coconut milk
2 tbsp peanut butter
2 scallions, roughly chopped
*1 fresh red chili, deseeded
   and sliced*

1 Grease and line a pan measuring 8 × 4 × 1 inches.

2 ▼ To make the sauce, put the garlic, salt, peppercorns, cilantro, and lemon juice into a mortar and pestle, or blender. Grind finely.

3 ▼ Add the coconut milk, peanut butter, scallions, and chili. Grind finely. Transfer to a saucepan and bring to a boil. Let cool. This sauce will keep well for 3–5 days in a refrigerator.

4 To cook the rice, do not rinse. Bring the water to a boil and add the rice. Stir and return to a medium boil. Cook, uncovered, for 14–16 minutes, until very soft. Drain thoroughly.

5 Put ⅔ cup of the cooked rice in a blender and combine. Alternatively, grind to a paste in a mortar and pestle.

6 ▼ Stir the ground rice into the remaining cooked rice and spoon into the lined pan. Level the surface and cover with plastic wrap. Compress the rice by using either a similar-size of pan, which will fit into the filled pan, or a small piece of board, and weigh this down with food cans or kitchen scale weights. Chill the rice in the refrigerator for at least 8 hours, or preferably overnight.

7 Invert the pan onto a cutting board. Cut the rice into cubes with a wet knife. Serve the cubes with the cilantro dipping sauce.

MUSHROOM WONTONS WITH PIQUANT DIPPING SAUCE

Mushroom-filled crispy wontons are served on skewers with a dipping sauce flavored with chilies.

SERVES 4

INGREDIENTS:
8 wooden skewers
1 tbsp vegetable oil
1 tbsp chopped onion
1 small garlic clove, chopped
¼ tsp chopped fresh ginger
¼ cup chopped flat mushrooms
16 wonton skins (see page 29)
vegetable oil, for
*   deep-frying*
salt

PIQUANT
DIPPING SAUCE:
2 tbsp vegetable oil
2 scallions, shredded thinly
1 red and 1 green fresh chili, deseeded
*   and thinly shredded*
3 tbsp light soy sauce
1 tbsp vinegar
1 tbsp dry sherry
pinch of sugar

1 ▲ Heat the oil in a wok or skillet. Add the onion, garlic, and ginger, and stir-fry for 2 minutes. Stir in the mushrooms and fry for another 2 minutes. Season well with salt and let cool.

2 ▲ Place 1 teaspoon of the cooled mushroom filling in the center of each wonton skin. Bring two opposite corners together to cover the mixture and pinch together to seal. Repeat with the remaining corners.

3 Thread 2 wontons onto each skewer. Heat enough oil in a large saucepan to deep-fry the wontons in batches until they are golden and crisp. Remove with a perforated spoon and drain on paper towels.

4 To make the sauce, first heat the oil in a small saucepan until quite hot. To test the oil, drop a small cube of bread in the oil; if it browns in a few seconds, the oil is the correct temperature.

5 ▲ Put the shredded scallions and chilies in a bowl and pour the hot oil slowly on top. Then stir in the remaining sauce ingredients, mixing well, and serve with the crispy mushroom wontons.

CRISPY-FRIED VEGETABLES WITH HOT & SWEET DIPPING SAUCE

A Thai-style sauce makes the perfect accompaniment to fried vegetables.

SERVES 4

✿✿✿✿✿✿✿✿✿✿✿✿✿✿✿

INGREDIENTS:
vegetable oil, for deep-frying
1 pound selection of raw
   vegetables, such as cauliflower,
   broccoli, mushrooms, zucchini, bell
   peppers, and baby corn, cut
   into pieces

BATTER:
1 cup all-purpose flour
½ tsp salt
1 tsp superfine sugar
1 tsp baking powder
3 tbsp vegetable oil
scant 1 cup warm water

SAUCE:
6 tbsp cider vinegar
2 tbsp Thai fish sauce or light soy sauce
2 tbsp water
1 tbsp brown sugar
pinch of salt
2 garlic cloves, crushed
2 tsp grated fresh ginger
2 fresh red chilies, deseeded and
   chopped
2 tbsp chopped fresh cilantro

✿✿✿✿✿✿✿✿✿✿✿✿✿✿✿

1 ▼ To make the batter, sift the flour, salt, sugar, and baking powder into a large bowl. Add the oil and most of the water. Whisk together to make a smooth batter, adding extra water to give it the consistency of cream. Refrigerate for 20–30 minutes.

2 ▼ Meanwhile, make the sauce. Heat the vinegar, fish sauce or soy sauce, water, sugar, and salt until boiling. Remove from the heat and let cool.

3 Mix together the garlic, ginger, chilies, and cilantro in a small serving bowl. Pour over the cooled vinegar mixture and stir together well to combine.

4 ▼ Heat the oil for deep-frying in a wok or deep-fat fryer to about 350–375°F, or until a cube of bread browns in 30 seconds. Dip the prepared vegetables in the batter and fry them, a few at a time, until crisp and golden – about 2 minutes. Drain on paper towels.

5 Serve the vegetables accompanied by the dipping sauce.

BUTTERFLY SHRIMP

For this recipe, use large, unpeeled, raw colossal or jumbo shrimp, about 3–4 inches long.

SERVES 4

INGREDIENTS:
12 raw colossal or jumbo shrimp in their shells
2 tbsp light soy sauce
1 tbsp Chinese rice wine or dry sherry
1 tbsp cornstarch
2 eggs, lightly beaten
8–10 tbsp breadcrumbs
vegetable oil, for deep-frying
salt and pepper
shredded lettuce leaves, to serve
chopped scallions, to garnish

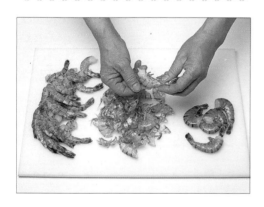

1 ▲ Shell the shrimp, but leave the tails on. Devein by making a shallow cut along the back of each shrimp, then pull out the black vein.

2 ▼ Split them in half from the underbelly, about halfway along, leaving the tails still firmly attached.

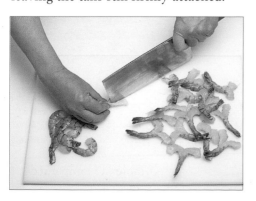

3 Mix together the salt, pepper, soy sauce, wine, and cornstarch in a bowl. Add the shrimp and turn to coat evenly. Let marinate for 10–15 minutes.

4 ▼ Pick up each shrimp by the tail, dip it in the beaten egg, then roll it in the breadcrumbs to coat it all over.

5 Heat the oil in a wok or deep-fat fryer to about 350–375°F, or until a cube of bread browns in 30 seconds. Deep-fry the shrimp in batches until golden brown. Remove them from the oil with a perforated spoon and drain on paper towels.

6 To serve, arrange the shrimp neatly on a bed of lettuce leaves and garnish with the scallions, either raw or soaked for about 30 seconds in hot oil.

PORK SATAY

This is the classic satay, which can also be made with chicken. Here the slivers of pork make delicate skewers, which will cook quickly.

SERVES 6–8

INGREDIENTS:

36 wooden skewers, soaked in
    hand-hot water for 20 minutes
2 pounds pork (loin or leg end steaks)
1 small onion, sliced finely
2 garlic cloves, crushed
1 tsp ground coriander
1 tsp ground cumin
2 fresh red chilies, deseeded and
    chopped
1-inch piece fresh ginger, grated
2 tbsp soy sauce
2 tbsp oil
1 tbsp lemon juice
1 tsp brown sugar

PEANUT SAUCE:

1 small onion, quartered
3 garlic cloves, crushed
½ tsp ground coriander
½ tsp ground cumin
1 tbsp lemon juice
1 tsp salt
½ fresh red chili, deseeded and
    sliced
½ cup coconut milk
1 cup crunchy peanut butter
1 cup water

1 ▼ Cut the pork into thin slivers, about 5 inches long and ½ inch thick. Put the slices into a nonporous dish.

2 ▲ Combine the onion, garlic, coriander, cumin, chilies, ginger, soy sauce, oil, lemon juice, and brown sugar. Pour over the pork, and stir to make sure that it is evenly coated. Let marinate for 2–3 hours.

3 Meanwhile, make the peanut sauce. Chop the onion finely by hand or feed it through the tube of a food processor. Then add the remaining ingredients in order, except for the water, and combine thoroughly.

4 Transfer the sauce mixture to a saucepan and add the water. Bring to a boil and cook until the desired thickness is reached. Set aside.

5 ▼ Thread the pork slivers onto the soaked skewers in an "S" shape.

6 Cook over a medium grill or under a preheated hot broiler for 10 minutes, turning frequently. Serve the skewers hot or cold, accompanied by the peanut sauce.

DEEP-FRIED SPARE RIBS

The spare ribs should be chopped into small bite-size pieces before or after cooking.

SERVES 4

INGREDIENTS:
8–10 finger-size spare ribs
1 tsp five-spice powder, or 1 tbsp mild curry powder
1 tbsp Chinese rice wine or dry sherry
1 egg
2 tbsp flour
vegetable oil, for deep-frying
1 tsp finely shredded scallions
1 tsp finely shredded fresh green or red chilies, deseeded
salt and pepper

SPICY SALT AND PEPPER
1 tbsp salt
1 tsp ground Szechuan peppercorns
1 tsp five-spice powder

1 Mix all the ingredients for the spicy salt and pepper together. Place in a dry skillet and stir-fry for 3–4 minutes over a low heat, stirring constantly. Let cool.

2 ▼ Chop the ribs into 3–4 small pieces. Place the ribs in a bowl with salt, pepper, five-spice or curry powder, and the wine. Turn to coat the ribs in the spices and let them marinate for 1–2 hours.

3 Mix the egg and flour together to make a batter.

4 ▼ Dip the ribs in the batter one by one to coat well.

5 Heat the oil in a preheated wok until smoking and the temperature reaches about 350–375°F. Deep-fry the ribs for 4–5 minutes, then remove them with a perforated spoon and drain on paper towels.

6 ▼ Reheat the oil over a high heat and deep-fry the ribs once more for another minute. Remove and drain again on paper towels.

7 Pour 1 tablespoon of the hot oil over the scallions and chilies and leave for 30–40 seconds. Garnish the ribs with the shredded scallions and chilies, and serve with the spicy salt and pepper for dipping.

LITTLE GOLDEN PACKAGES

These little packages will draw admiring gasps from your guests, but they are fairly simple to prepare.

MAKES 30

INGREDIENTS:
1 garlic clove, crushed
1 tsp chopped cilantro root
1 tsp pepper
1 cup mashed potato
1 cup finely chopped water
    chestnuts
1 tsp grated fresh ginger
2 tbsp ground roasted peanuts
2 tsp light soy sauce
½ tsp salt
½ tsp sugar
30 wonton skins, defrosted
1 tsp cornstarch, made into a
    paste with a little water
    (see page 15)
vegetable oil, for deep-frying
fresh chives, to garnish
sweet chili sauce, to serve

1 ▼ Combine all the ingredients thoroughly, except the wonton skins, cornstarch paste, and oil.

2 Keeping the rest of the wonton skins covered with a damp cloth, lay 4 skins out on a work counter.

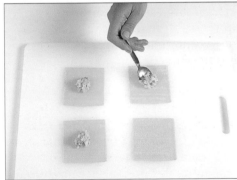

3 ▲ Put a teaspoonful of the mixture on each wonton skin.

4 ▼ Make a line of the cornstarch paste around each skin, about ½ inch from the edge.

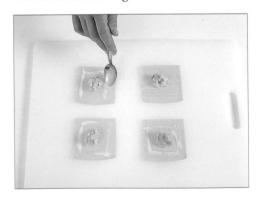

5 ▼ For each skin, bring all 4 corners to the center and press together to form a little bag. Continue the process of filling and wrapping until all the wonton skins are used.

6 Meanwhile, heat 2 inches of the vegetable oil in a deep saucepan until a light haze appears on top. Lower the wonton packages in, in batches of 3. Fry until golden brown, remove with a perforated spoon, and drain on paper towels.

7 Tie a chive around the neck of each package to garnish, and serve with the sweet chili sauce for dipping.

MONEY BAGS

These steamed dumplings are made with a mushroom and corn filling. Eat them as they are, or try dipping them in a mixture of soy sauce, sherry, and slivers of fresh ginger.

SERVES 4

INGREDIENTS:
3 Chinese dried mushrooms (if unavailable, use thinly sliced open-cup mushrooms)
2 tbsp vegetable oil
2 scallions, chopped
¼ cup canned corn kernels
¼ fresh red chili, deseeded and chopped
1 tbsp brown bean sauce

WRAPPERS:
2 cups all-purpose flour
1 egg, beaten
¼ cup water
1 tsp baking powder
¼ tsp salt

1 Place the dried mushrooms in a small bowl, cover with warm water, and let soak for 20–25 minutes.

2 ▼ Meanwhile make the wrappers. Sift the flour into a bowl, add the egg, and mix in lightly. Stir in the water, baking powder, and salt. Mix to make a soft dough. Knead lightly until smooth on a floured board. Cover with a damp cloth and set aside for 5–6 minutes. This allows the baking powder time to activate, so the dumplings swell when steaming.

3 Drain the soaked mushrooms, squeezing them dry. Remove the tough centers and chop the mushrooms.

4 Heat the vegetable oil in a wok or large skillet and stir-fry the mushrooms, scallions, corn kernels, and chili for about 2 minutes. Stir in the brown bean sauce to coat the vegetables, then remove the mixture from the heat.

5 ▼ Roll the dough into a large sausage and cut into 24 even-size pieces. Roll each piece out into a thin round and place a teaspoonful of the mushroom and corn filling in the center.

6 ▼ Gather up the edges to a point, pinch together, and twist to seal.

7 ▼ Stand the dumplings in an oiled bamboo steamer. Place over a pan of simmering water, cover, and steam for 12–14 minutes before serving.

NOODLE, MUSHROOM, & GINGER SOUP

Thai soups are very quickly and easily put together, and are cooked so each ingredient can still be tasted, even after it has been combined with several others.

SERVES 4

INGREDIENTS:
¼ cup dried Chinese mushrooms,
   or 1¼ cups wild mushrooms, such as
   field or crimini
4 cups hot vegetable stock
4 ounces thread egg
   noodles
2 tsp sunflower oil
3 garlic cloves, crushed
1-inch piece fresh ginger,
   finely shredded
¼ tsp mushroom ketchup
1 tsp light soy sauce
2 cups bean sprouts
cilantro leaves,
   to garnish

1 Soak the dried Chinese mushrooms, if using, for at least 30 minutes in 1¼ cups of the vegetable stock. Remove the stalks and discard, then slice the mushrooms. Reserve the stock.

2 Cook the noodles for 2–3 minutes in boiling water. Drain and rinse. Set them aside.

3 ▼ Heat the oil over a high heat in a wok or large, heavy skillet. Add the garlic and ginger, stir, and add the mushrooms. Stir over a high heat for 2 minutes.

4 ▼ Add the remaining vegetable stock to the wok or skillet, along with the reserved vegetable stock from the mushrooms, and bring to a boil. Add the mushroom ketchup and soy sauce.

5 ▼ Stir in the bean sprouts and cook until tender.

6 Spoon the soup over the noodles, garnish with cilantro leaves, and serve immediately.

LETTUCE & BEAN CURD SOUP

This is a delicate, clear soup of shredded lettuce and small chunks of bean curd, with sliced carrot and scallion.

SERVES 4

INGREDIENTS:
7 ounces bean curd
2 tbsp vegetable oil
1 carrot, sliced thinly
¼-inch piece fresh ginger, cut into thin shreds
3 scallions, sliced diagonally
5 cups vegetable stock
2 tbsp soy sauce
2 tbsp dry sherry
1 tsp sugar
1½ cups shredded romaine lettuce
salt and pepper

1 ▼ Cut the bean curd into small cubes. Heat the oil in a wok or large saucepan, add the bean curd, and stir fry until browned. Remove with a perforated spoon and drain on paper towels.

2 ▲ Add the carrot, fresh ginger, and scallions to the wok or saucepan. Stir-fry for 2 minutes.

3 Add the stock, soy sauce, sherry, and sugar. Bring to a boil and simmer for 1 minute.

4 ▼ Add the lettuce and stir until it has just wilted.

5 Return the bean curd to the wok or saucepan to reheat. Season with salt and pepper, and serve in warmed bowls.

THAI-STYLE CHICKEN & COCONUT SOUP

*This fragrant soup has the complex
flavors so typical of Thai food.
It combines the citrus flavors of
lemon grass and lime with coconut,
and a hint of piquancy comes from
the fresh red chilies.*

SERVES 4

INGREDIENTS:

*8 ounces cooked, skinned chicken
     breast*
*1⅓ cups unsweetened shredded
     coconut*
2 cups boiling water
2 cups chicken stock
*4 scallions, white and green parts,
     sliced thinly*
2 lemon grass stalks
1 lime
1 tsp grated fresh ginger
1 tbsp light soy sauce
2 tsp ground coriander
2 large fresh red chilies
1 tbsp chopped fresh cilantro
*1 tbsp cornstarch, mixed with 2 tbsp
     cold water*
salt and white pepper
*chopped fresh red chili,
     to garnish*

1 ▼ Slice the chicken into thin strips.
Place the coconut in a heatproof bowl
and pour the boiling water over.

2 ▲ Place a fine strainer over another
bowl and pour in the coconut water.
Work the coconut through the strainer.
Pour the coconut water into a large
saucepan and add the stock.

3 ▲ Add the scallions to the saucepan.
Slice the base of each lemon grass stalk
and discard any damaged leaves.
Bruise the stalks and add to
the saucepan.

4 Peel the rind from the whole lime,
keeping it in large strips. Slice the lime
in half and extract the juice. Add the
lime strips, lime juice, grated ginger,
soy sauce, and ground coriander to
the saucepan.

5 ▲ Bruise the chilies with a fork, then
add them to the saucepan. Heat the
contents of the pan to just below the
boiling point.

6 Add the chicken strips and fresh
cilantro to the saucepan. Bring to a
boil, then simmer for about
10 minutes.

7 Discard the lemon grass, lime rind,
and chilies. Pour the blended
cornstarch mixture into the saucepan
and stir until slightly thickened.
Season to taste, then serve, garnished
with chopped red chili.

HOT & SOUR SOUP

A very traditional staple of the Thai national diet, and quite different from the Chinese soup of the same name, this soup is sold on street corners, at food bars, and by mobile vendors all over Thailand.

SERVES 4

INGREDIENTS:
1 tbsp sunflower oil
8 ounces smoked bean curd, sliced
1 cup sliced shiitake mushrooms
2 tbsp chopped fresh cilantro
2 cups watercress
1 fresh red chili, sliced finely, to garnish

STOCK:
1 tbsp tamarind pulp
2 dried red chilies, chopped
2 kaffir lime leaves, torn in half
1-inch piece fresh ginger, chopped
2-inch piece galangal, chopped
1 lemon grass stalk, chopped
1 onion, quartered
4 cups cold water

1 ▼ Put all the ingredients for the stock into a saucepan and bring to a boil. Simmer for 5 minutes. Remove the pan from the heat and strain, reserving the stock.

2 ▼ Heat the oil in a wok or large, heavy skillet and cook the bean curd over a high heat for about 2 minutes, stirring constantly. Add the strained stock.

3 ▼ Add the mushrooms and cilantro, and boil for 3 minutes. Add the watercress and boil for 1 minute more. Serve immediately, garnished with red chili slices.

CORN & CRABMEAT SOUP

You must use canned creamed corn for this soup to produce the correct texture and taste. Chicken can be substituted for the crabmeat, if preferred.

SERVES 4

INGREDIENTS:
4 ounces crabmeat
¼ tsp finely chopped fresh
   ginger
2 egg whites
2 tbsp milk
1 tbsp cornstarch paste
   (see page 15)
2 ½ cups Chinese Stock
   (see page 10)
8-ounce can creamed corn
salt and pepper
finely chopped scallions,
   to garnish

1 Flake the crabmeat (or coarsely chop the chicken breast) and mix it with the ginger.

2 ▼ Beat the egg whites until frothy, add the milk and cornstarch paste, and beat again until smooth. Blend in the crabmeat or chicken.

3 ▲ In a wok or large skillet, bring the stock to a boil, add the creamed corn, and bring back to a boil.

4 ▼ Stir in the crabmeat or chicken pieces and the egg-white mixture. Adjust the seasoning and stir gently until the mixture is well blended. Serve hot, garnished with chopped scallions.

WONTON SOUP

Wontons filled with spinach and pine nuts are served in a clear soup. The recipe for the wonton skins makes 24, but the soup requires only half this quantity. The other half can be frozen, to be used another time.

SERVES 4

INGREDIENTS:
WONTON SKINS:
1 egg
6 tbsp water
2 cups all-purpose flour

FILLING:
¼ cup chopped frozen spinach, defrosted
1 tbsp toasted and chopped pine nuts
¼ cup ground TVP (texturized vegetable protein) or soy granules
salt

SOUP:
2¼ cups vegetable stock
1 tbsp dry sherry
1 tbsp light soy sauce
2 scallions, chopped

1 ▼ Beat the egg lightly in a bowl and mix with the water. Stir in the flour to form a stiff dough. Knead lightly, then cover with a damp dish cloth and let stand for 30 minutes.

2 Roll the dough out into a large sheet, about ¼ inch thick. Cut out 24 3-inch squares. Dust each one lightly with flour. Only 12 squares are needed for the soup, so freeze the rest for using another time.

3 ▲ To make the filling, squeeze out the excess water from the frozen spinach. Mix the spinach with the pine nuts and TVP or soy granules. Season with salt.

4 ▲ Divide the mixture into 12 equal portions and place one portion in the center of each square. Seal by bringing the opposite corners of each square together and squeezing well.

5 To make the soup, bring the stock, sherry, and soy sauce to a boil. Add the wontons, and boil rapidly for 2–3 minutes. Add the scallions and serve the soup immediately in warmed bowls.

THREE-FLAVOR SOUP

Ideally, use raw shrimp in this delicious soup. If that is not possible, add cooked shrimp at the very last stage of cooking.

SERVES 4

INGREDIENTS:
*4 ounces skinned, boned chicken
    breast
4 ounces raw, peeled shrimp
4 ounces honey-glazed ham
½ egg white, lightly beaten
2 tsp cornstarch paste
    (see page 15)
3 cups Chinese Stock (see page 10) or
    water
salt and pepper
finely chopped scallions,
    to garnish*

1 ▲ Thinly slice the chicken into small shreds. If the shrimp are large, cut each in half lengthwise; otherwise, leave whole.

2 ▲ Cut the ham into thin slices, roughly the same size as the chicken.

3 ▼ Place the sliced chicken and shrimp in a mixing bowl. Add a pinch of salt, the egg white, and the cornstarch paste and mix until well coated.

4 Bring the stock or water to a rolling boil.

5 ▼ Add the chicken, the raw shrimp, and the ham to the stock. Bring the soup back to a boil, and simmer for 1 minute.

6 Adjust the seasoning and serve the soup hot, garnished with the chopped scallions.

NOODLE & RICE DISHES

Rice may well be the staple food in the East, but freshly cooked plain long-grain rice is only one way of serving it. In countless other dishes, it is baked, steamed, stir-fried, and boiled with an almost infinite spectrum of vegetables, herbs, spices, and flavorings to entice and delight. Noodles, too, have a major role to play, and many, simply fried with just a few extra ingredients, make superb light meals to enjoy in their own right. Noodles are served throughout the day, even for breakfast, and can be boiled, deep-fried, stir-fried with vegetables or meat, served with a sauce, or cooked in a soup. Some of the following recipes make ideal side dishes to accompany a more substantial main dish of meat or fish, whereas others would make a meal in themselves, such as the Singapore-Style Rice Noodles or the Seafood Chow Mein. In China, fried rice and chow mein are only served at formal occasions or as a snack between main meals, but there is no need for the Western cook to follow oriental customs so exactly – try serving both a rice and a noodle dish at a meal.

CHATUCHAK FRIED RICE (PAGE 46)

SINGAPORE-STYLE RICE NOODLES

Rice noodles or vermicelli are also known as rice sticks. Egg noodles can be used for this dish, but it will not taste the same.

SERVES 4

INGREDIENTS:

7 ounces rice vermicelli
4 ounces cooked chicken or pork
2 ounces peeled, cooked shrimp, defrosted if frozen
4 tbsp vegetable oil
1 medium onion, thinly shredded
2 cups fresh bean sprouts
1 tsp salt
1 tbsp mild curry powder
2 tbsp light soy sauce
2 scallions, shredded
1–2 small fresh green or red chilies, deseeded and shredded

1 ▲ Soak the rice vermicelli in boiling water for 8–10 minutes, then rinse in cold water and drain well.

2 ▼ Thinly slice the cooked meat. Dry the shrimp on paper towels.

3 ▲ Heat the oil in a preheated wok. Add the onion and stir-fry until opaque. Add the bean sprouts and stir-fry for 1 minute.

4 ▲ Add the noodles with the meat and shrimp, and continue stirring for another minute.

5 Blend in the salt, curry powder, and soy sauce, followed by the scallions and chilies. Stir-fry for one more minute, then serve immediately.

CRISPY DEEP-FRIED NOODLES

This is the staple dish on every Thai restaurant menu by which the establishment will be judged. It does require a certain amount of care and attention to get the crispy noodles properly cooked.

SERVES 4

❀❀❀❀❀❀❀❀❀❀❀❀❀❀❀❀❀❀❀

INGREDIENTS:

6 ounces thread egg noodles
2¼ cups sunflower oil,
   for deep-frying
2 tsp grated lemon rind
1 tbsp light soy sauce
1 tbsp rice vinegar
1 tbsp lemon juice
1¼ tbsp sugar
1 cup diced marinated
   bean curd
2 garlic cloves, crushed
1 fresh red chili, sliced finely
1 red bell pepper, diced
4 eggs, beaten
sliced fresh red chili, to garnish

❀❀❀❀❀❀❀❀❀❀❀❀❀❀❀❀❀❀❀

1 ▼ Blanch the egg noodles briefly in hot water, to which a little of the oil has been added. Drain and spread out to dry for at least 30 minutes. Cut into threads about 3 inches long.

2 Combine the lemon rind, light soy sauce, rice vinegar, lemon juice, and sugar in a small bowl.

3 ▲ Heat the oil in a wok or large, heavy skillet, and test the temperature with a few strands of noodles. They should swell to many times their size, but if they do not, wait until the oil is hot enough; otherwise, they will be tough and stringy, not puffy and light. Cook them in batches. As soon as they turn a pale gold color, scoop them out and drain on plenty of paper towels. Let cool.

4 ▼ Reserve 2 tablespoons of the oil and drain off the rest. Heat the 2 tablespoons of oil in the wok or skillet. Cook the bean curd quickly over a high heat to seal. Add the garlic, chili, and diced bell pepper. Stir for 1–2 minutes. Add the vinegar mixture to the skillet, stir, then add the eggs, stirring until they are set.

5 Serve with the crispy fried noodles, garnished with sliced red chili.

ORIENTAL VEGETABLE NOODLES

This dish has a mild, nutty flavor from the peanut butter and dry-roasted peanuts.

SERVES 4

INGREDIENTS:
6 ounces green thread noodles or multicolored spaghetti
1 cup grated daikon
1 large carrot, grated
1 cup finely shredded cucumber
1 bunch scallions, finely shredded
1 tbsp crushed dry-roasted peanuts

PEANUT DRESSING:
1 tsp sesame oil
2 tbsp crunchy peanut butter
2 tbsp light soy sauce
1 tbsp white wine vinegar
1 tsp clear honey
salt and pepper

TO GARNISH:
carrot flowers
scallion tassels

1 ▼ Bring a large saucepan of water to a boil, add the noodles or spaghetti, and cook according to the instructions on the package. Drain well and rinse in cold water. Leave in a bowl of cold water until needed.

2 Make the dressing. Put the sesame oil, peanut butter, soy sauce, vinegar, honey, and seasoning into a small screw-top jar. Seal and shake well.

3 ▼ Drain the noodles or spaghetti well, place in a large serving bowl, and mix in half the peanut dressing.

4 ▼ Using 2 forks, toss the daikon, carrot, cucumber, and scallions into the bowl.

5 Sprinkle with crushed peanuts and garnish with carrot flowers and scallion tassels. Serve with the remaining peanut dressing.

HOMEMADE NOODLES WITH STIR-FRIED VEGETABLES

These noodles are simple to make; you do not need a pasta-making machine or any specialist equipment because the noodles are rolled out by hand.

SERVES 2–4

INGREDIENTS:
NOODLES:
1 cup all-purpose flour
2 tbsp cornstarch
½ tsp salt
½ cup boiling water
5 tbsp vegetable oil

STIR-FRY:
1 zucchini
1 celery stalk
1 carrot
4 ounces open-cup mushrooms
1 leek
4 ounces broccoli
2 cups fresh bean sprouts
1 tbsp soy sauce
2 tsp rice vinegar (if unavailable, use white wine vinegar)
½ tsp sugar

1 ▼ To prepare the noodles, sift the flour, cornstarch, and salt into a large mixing bowl. Make a well in the center. Pour in the boiling water and 1 teaspoon of the oil. Mix quickly, using a wooden spoon, to make a soft dough. Cover and leave for 5–6 minutes.

2 Prepare the vegetables for the stir-fry. Cut the zucchini, celery, and carrot into thin sticks. Slice the mushrooms and leek. Divide the broccoli into small florets, then peel and thinly slice the stalks.

3 ▲ Make the noodles by breaking off small pieces of dough and rolling into balls. Then roll each ball across a very lightly oiled work counter with the palm of your hand to form thin noodles. Do not worry if some of the noodles break into shorter lengths. Set the noodles aside.

4 Heat 3 tablespoons of oil in a wok or large skillet. Add the noodles in batches and fry over a high heat for 1 minute. Reduce the heat and cook for another 2 minutes. Remove and drain on paper towels. Set aside.

5 ▼ Heat the remaining oil in the pan. Add the zucchini, celery, and carrot, and stir-fry for 1 minute. Add the mushrooms, broccoli, and leek, and stir-fry for another minute. Stir in the remaining ingredients and mix well until thoroughly heated.

6 Add the noodles and toss to mix over a high heat. Serve immediately.

SESAME HOT NOODLES

Plain egg noodles are all the better when tossed in a dressing made with nutty sesame oil, soy sauce, peanut butter, cilantro, lime juice, chili, and sesame seeds. Serve hot as an accompaniment to a main meal.

SERVES 6

INGREDIENTS:
*2 x 8-ounce packages medium
    egg noodles
3 tbsp sunflower oil
2 tbsp sesame oil
1 garlic clove, crushed
1 tbsp smooth peanut butter
1 small fresh green chili, deseeded and
    very finely chopped
3 tbsp toasted sesame seeds
4 tbsp light soy sauce
1–2 tbsp lime juice
salt and pepper
4 tbsp chopped fresh
    cilantro*

1 ▼ Place the noodles in a large pan of boiling water, then immediately remove from the heat. Cover and let stand for 6 minutes, stirring once halfway through. At the end of 6 minutes, the noodles will be perfectly cooked. Otherwise, follow the instructions on the package.

2 Meanwhile, mix the sunflower and sesame oils with the garlic and peanut butter until smooth.

3 ▼ Add the chili, sesame seeds, soy sauce, and lime juice, according to taste, and mix well. Season with salt and pepper.

4 ▼ Drain the noodles well, then place in a large heated serving bowl. Add the peanut dressing and fresh cilantro, and toss well to mix. Serve immediately.

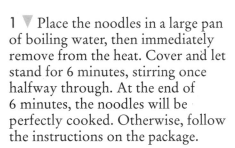

FRIED NOODLES WITH BEAN SPROUTS, CHIVES, & CHILI

This is a simple idea to jazz up noodles to accompany Thai or other oriental main-course dishes.

SERVES 4

INGREDIENTS:
1 pound medium egg noodles
1 cup fresh bean sprouts
¼ ounce chives
3 tbsp sunflower oil
1 garlic clove, crushed
4 fresh green chilies, deseeded, sliced, and soaked in 2 tbsp rice vinegar
salt

1 ▼ To cook the noodles, soak in boiling water for 10 minutes. Drain and set aside.

2 ▼ Soak the bean sprouts in cold water while you snip the chives into 1-inch pieces. Set a few chives aside for the garnish. Drain the bean sprouts thoroughly.

3 Heat the oil in a wok or large, heavy-based skillet. Add the crushed garlic and stir briefly.

4 ▼ Add the chilies to the wok or skillet and stir until fragrant, for about 1 minute.

5 ▲ Add the bean sprouts, stir, and then add the noodles. Stir in some salt and the chives. Using 2 spoons, lift and stir the noodles for 1 minute.

6 Garnish the finished dish with the reserved chives, and serve at once.

SEAFOOD CHOW MEIN

Use whatever seafood is available for this delicious noodle dish – mussels or crab would also be suitable. Simply add to the wok with the other seafood in step 6.

SERVES 4

❀❀❀❀❀❀❀❀❀❀❀❀❀

INGREDIENTS:

3 ounces squid
3–4 fresh scallops
3 ounces raw shrimp,
  shelled
⅓ egg white, lightly beaten
1 tbsp cornstarch paste
  (see page 15)
9 ounces egg noodles
5–6 tbsp vegetable oil
2 tbsp light soy sauce
⅓ cup trimmed snow peas
⅓ tsp salt
⅓ tsp sugar
1 tsp Chinese rice wine or
  dry sherry
2 scallions, finely shredded
few drops of sesame oil

❀❀❀❀❀❀❀❀❀❀❀❀❀

1 First clean the squid. Cut off the head. Cut off the tentacles and reserve. Remove the small bone at the base of the tentacles and the transparent backbone, as well as the ink bag. Peel off the thin skin, then wash and dry.

2 ▼ Open up the squid and score the inside in a crisscross pattern, then cut into pieces about the size of a large postage stamp.

3 ▼ Soak the squid in a bowl of boiling water until all the pieces curl up. Rinse in cold water and drain.

4 Cut each scallop into 3–4 slices. Cut the shrimp in half lengthwise if they are large ones. Mix the sliced scallops and shrimp with the egg white and cornstarch paste in a mixing bowl.

5 Cook the noodles in boiling water according to the instructions on the package, then drain and rinse under cold water. Drain well, then toss with about 1 tablespoon of oil.

6 ▼ Heat 3 tablespoons of oil in a preheated wok. Add the noodles and 1 tablespoon of the soy sauce, and stir-fry for 2–3 minutes. Transfer to a large serving dish.

7 Heat the remaining oil in the wok and add the snow peas and seafood. Stir-fry for about 2 minutes, then add the salt, sugar, wine, remaining soy sauce, and about half the scallions. Blend well, and add a little stock or water if necessary.

8 Pour the seafood mixture on top of the noodles and sprinkle with sesame oil. Garnish with the remaining scallions and serve hot or cold.

EGG FU-YUNG WITH RICE

In this dish, cooked rice is mixed with scrambled eggs, Chinese mushrooms, bamboo shoots, and water chestnuts, and it is a great way of using up leftover cooked rice. It can be served as a meal by itself or as an accompaniment.

SERVES 2–4

INGREDIENTS:

generous ¾ cup long-grain rice
2 Chinese dried mushrooms (if unavailable, use thinly sliced open-cup mushrooms)
3 eggs, beaten
3 tbsp vegetable oil
4 scallions, sliced
¼ green bell pepper, chopped
¼ cup drained canned bamboo shoots
¼ cup sliced, drained canned water chestnuts
2 cups bean sprouts
2 tbsp light soy sauce
2 tbsp dry sherry
2 tsp sesame oil
salt and pepper

1 Cook the rice in lightly salted boiling water according to the instructions on the package.

2 ▲ Place the dried mushrooms in a small bowl, cover with warm water, and soak for 20–25 minutes.

3 ▼ Mix the beaten eggs with a little salt. Heat 1 tablespoon of the oil in a wok or large skillet. Add the eggs and stir until they are just set. Remove and set aside.

4 Drain the mushrooms and squeeze out the excess water. Remove the tough centers and chop the mushrooms.

5 Heat the remaining oil in a clean wok or skillet. Add the mushrooms, scallions, and green bell pepper, and stir-fry for 2 minutes. Add the bamboo shoots, water chestnuts, and bean sprouts. Stir-fry for another minute.

6 ▲ Drain the rice well and add to the wok or skillet with the remaining ingredients. Mix well, heating the rice thoroughly. Season to taste with salt and pepper. Stir in the reserved eggs and serve.

FRAGRANT STEAMED RICE IN LOTUS LEAVES

The fragrance of the leaves penetrates the rice, giving it a unique taste. Lotus leaves can be bought from specialist oriental markets. Large cabbage or spinach leaves can be used as a substitute.

SERVES 4

INGREDIENTS:
2 lotus leaves
4 Chinese dried mushrooms (if unavailable, use thinly sliced open-cup mushrooms)
generous $\frac{3}{4}$ cup long-grain rice
1 cinnamon stick
6 cardamom pods
4 cloves
1 tsp salt
2 eggs
1 tbsp vegetable oil
2 scallions, chopped
1 tbsp soy sauce
2 tbsp sherry
1 tsp sugar
1 tsp sesame oil

1 ▼ Unfold the lotus leaves carefully and cut along the fold to divide each lotus leaf in half. Lay on a large baking sheet and pour over enough hot water to cover. Let soak for about 30 minutes, or until the lotus leaves have softened.

2 Place the dried mushrooms in a small bowl and cover with warm water. Let the mushrooms soak for 20–25 minutes.

3 Cook the long-grain rice in plenty of boiling water in a saucepan with the cinnamon stick, cardamom pods, cloves, and salt for about 10 minutes – the rice should be partially cooked. Drain thoroughly and remove the cinnamon stick.

4 ▲ In a mixing bowl, lightly beat the eggs. Heat the oil in a wok or skillet and cook the eggs quickly, stirring constantly until set; then remove and set aside.

5 Drain the mushrooms, squeezing out the excess water. Remove the tough centers and chop the mushrooms.

6 Place the drained rice in a large bowl. Stir in the chopped mushrooms, cooked egg, scallions, soy sauce, sherry, sugar, and sesame oil. Season with salt to taste.

7 ▼ Drain the lotus leaves and divide the rice mixture into four portions. Place a portion in the center of each lotus leaf and fold up to form a "package."

8 Place the lotus leaf "packages" in a bamboo steamer, cover, and steam over simmering water for 20 minutes. To serve, cut the tops of the lotus leaves open to expose the fragrant rice inside. ◆

THAI FRAGRANT COCONUT RICE

This is the finest rice to serve with Thai-style food. Basmati rice is cooked with creamed coconut, lemon grass, fresh ginger, and spices to make a wonderfully aromatic, fluffy rice. When using lemon grass, beat it well to bruise it before slicing or chopping so the flavor is fully released.

SERVES 4–6

INGREDIENTS:
*1-inch piece fresh ginger, peeled and
   sliced*
2 cloves
1 lemon grass stalk, bruised and halved
2 tsp ground nutmeg
1 cinnamon stick
1 bay leaf
2 small thin strips lime rind
1 tsp salt
1 ounce creamed coconut, chopped
2½ cups water
1¾ cups basmati rice
pepper

1 ▼ Place the ginger, cloves, lemon grass, nutmeg, cinnamon stick, bay leaf, lime rind, salt, creamed coconut, and water in a large, heavy-based saucepan and bring slowly to a boil.

2 ▼ Add the rice, stir well, then cover and simmer over a very gentle heat for about 15 minutes, or until all the liquid has been absorbed and the rice is tender but still has a bite to it.

3 ▲ Remove from the heat, add pepper to taste, then fluff up the rice with a fork. Remove the large pieces of spices before serving.

NASI GORENG

An Indonesian rice dish flavored with vegetables and pork, soy sauce, and curry spices, with strips of omelet added as a topping.

SERVES 4

INGREDIENTS:

1½ cups long-grain rice
about 1 pound pork fillet or lean
   pork slices
3 tomatoes, skinned, quartered, and
   deseeded
2 eggs
4 tsp water
3 tbsp sunflower oil
1 onion, thinly sliced
1–2 garlic cloves, crushed
1 tsp medium or mild curry powder
¼ tsp ground coriander
¼ tsp medium chili powder, or 1 tsp
   bottled sweet chili sauce
2 tbsp soy sauce
¾ cup frozen peas, defrosted
salt and pepper

1 Cook the rice in boiling, salted water, following the instructions on the package, and keep warm.

2 Meanwhile, cut the pork into narrow strips across the grain, discarding any fat. Slice the tomatoes.

3 ▲ Beat each egg separately with 2 teaspoons cold water and salt and pepper. Heat 2 teaspoons of oil in the wok, swirling it around until really hot. Pour in the first egg, swirl it around, and cook, undisturbed, until set.

4 Remove to a plate or cutting board and repeat with the second egg. Cut the omelets into strips, about ½ inch wide.

5 ▼ Heat the remaining oil in the wok. When it is really hot, add the onion and garlic and stir-fry for 1–2 minutes. Add the pork and continue to stir-fry for about 3 minutes, or until almost cooked.

6 Add the curry powder, coriander, chili powder or chili sauce, and soy sauce to the wok. Cook for another minute, stirring constantly.

7 ▲ Stir in the rice, tomatoes, and peas, and stir-fry for about 2 minutes until piping hot. Adjust the seasoning and transfer to a heated serving dish. Arrange the strips of omelet on top and serve at once.

GREEN RICE

A deliciously different way to serve plain rice for a special occasion or to liven up a simple meal.

SERVES 4

INGREDIENTS:
2 tbsp olive oil
2¼ cups basmati or Thai jasmine rice, soaked for 1 hour, rinsed, and drained
3 cups unsweetened coconut milk
1 tsp salt
1 bay leaf
2 tbsp chopped fresh cilantro
2 tbsp chopped fresh mint
2 fresh green chilies, deseeded and finely chopped

1 ▼ Heat the oil in a saucepan, add the rice, and stir until it becomes translucent.

2 ▲ Add the coconut milk, salt, and bay leaf. Bring to a boil and cook until all the liquid is absorbed.

3 ▼ Lower the heat as much as possible, cover the saucepan tightly, and cook for 10 minutes. Remove the bay leaf.

4 ▲ Stir in the chopped cilantro, mint, and green chilies. Fork through the rice gently and serve immediately.

SPECIAL FRIED RICE

In this simple recipe, cooked rice is fried with vegetables and cashews. It can either be eaten on its own or served as an accompaniment.

SERVES 2–4

INGREDIENTS:
generous ¼ cup long-grain rice
¼ cup cashews
1 carrot
1 cucumber
1 yellow bell pepper
2 scallions
2 tbsp vegetable oil
1 garlic clove, crushed
¼ cup frozen peas, defrosted
1 tbsp soy sauce
1 tsp salt
cilantro leaves,
*   to garnish*

1 Bring a large saucepan of water to a boil. Add the rice and simmer for 15 minutes. Tip the rice into a strainer and rinse well. Drain thoroughly.

2 ▲ Heat a wok or large skillet, add the cashews, and dry-fry until the nuts are lightly browned. Remove and set aside.

3 ▲ Cut the carrot in half along the length, then slice thinly into semicircles. Halve the cucumber and remove the seeds, using a teaspoon, then dice the cucumber. Slice the yellow bell pepper and chop the scallions.

4 ▼ Heat the oil in the wok or large skillet. Add the prepared vegetables and the garlic. Stir-fry for 3 minutes. Add the rice, peas, soy sauce, and salt. Continue to stir-fry until well mixed and heated through.

5 Stir in the reserved cashews and serve garnished with fresh cilantro leaves.

CHINESE FRIED RICE

The rice for this dish may be cooked in the wok or conventionally in a saucepan, but it is essential to use cold, dry rice with separate grains to make this recipe properly.

SERVES 4-6

INGREDIENTS:

3 cups water
½ tsp salt
1½ cups long-grain rice
2 eggs
4 tsp cold water
3 tbsp sunflower oil
*4 scallions, sliced
   diagonally*
*1 red, green, or yellow bell pepper,
   cored, deseeded, and thinly sliced*
*3-4 slices lean bacon, cut into
   strips*
3½ cups fresh bean sprouts
¾ cup frozen peas, defrosted
2 tbsp soy sauce (optional)
salt and pepper

1 Pour the water into the wok with the salt and bring to a boil. Rinse the rice in a strainer under cold water until the water runs clear. Drain well and add to the boiling water. Stir well, then cover the wok tightly with the lid or a lid made of foil, and simmer gently for 12–13 minutes. (Don't remove the lid during cooking.)

2 ▼ Remove the lid, give the rice a good stir, and then spread it out on a large plate, tray, or baking sheet to cool and dry.

3 Beat one egg in a small bowl with salt and pepper and 2 teaspoons cold water. Heat 1 tablespoon of the oil in the wok, swirling it around until really hot. Pour in the egg, swirl it around, and leave to cook undisturbed until set. Remove the cooked omelet to a cutting board or plate, and repeat the whole process with the second egg.

4 ▲ Roll up each omelet and cut it across into thin slices.

5 ▼ Add the remaining oil to the wok. When it is really hot, add the scallions and bell pepper, and stir-fry for 1–2 minutes. Add the bacon and continue to stir-fry for another 1–2 minutes. Add the bean sprouts and peas, and toss together thoroughly. Stir in the soy sauce, if using.

6 Add the rice and seasoning. Stir-fry for a minute or so, then add the strips of omelet and continue to stir for about 2 minutes, or until the rice is piping hot. Serve at once.

CHATUCHAK FRIED RICE

An excellent way to use up leftover rice! Freeze it as soon as it is cool. It will be ready to use at any time. This dish should be reheated only once.

SERVES 4

❁❁❁❁❁❁❁❁❁❁❁❁❁❁

INGREDIENTS:
1 tbsp sunflower oil
3 shallots, chopped finely
2 garlic cloves, crushed
1 fresh red chili, deseeded and finely chopped
1-inch piece fresh ginger, finely shredded
⧧ green bell pepper, finely sliced
2–3 baby eggplants, quartered
1 cup sugar snap peas or snow peas, trimmed and blanched
6 baby corn, halved lengthwise and blanched
1 tomato, cut into 8 pieces
1½ cups fresh bean sprouts
3 cups cooked Thai jasmine rice
2 tbsp tomato ketchup
2 tbsp light soy sauce

TO GARNISH:
cilantro leaves
lime wedges

❁❁❁❁❁❁❁❁❁❁❁❁❁❁

1 ▲ Heat the sunflower oil in a wok or large, heavy skillet over a high heat. Add the shallots, garlic, chili, and ginger. Stir until the shallots have softened.

2 Add the green bell pepper and baby eggplants, and stir.

3 ▼ Add the sugar snap peas or snow peas, baby corn, tomato pieces, and bean sprouts. Stir the vegetables for 3 minutes.

4 ▲ Add the rice, and lift and stir with 2 spoons for 4–5 minutes, until no more steam is released. Stir in the tomato ketchup and soy sauce.

5 Serve immediately, garnished with cilantro and lime wedges.

VEGETABLE &
VEGETARIAN DISHES

The oriental diet is rich in vegetables, and many meat and poultry dishes include some kind of vegetable as a supplementary ingredient. An astonishing range of vegetables is found in the East, many which are not available to Westerners, such as the numerous varieties of eggplant found in Thailand in every size, shape, and color. When selecting vegetables for cooking, choose very fresh ingredients, wash them just before cutting or chopping, then cook them as soon as they have been cut so the vitamin content is not lost. Some of the recipes in this chapter, such as the Green Curry with Tempeh or the Vegetable & Nut Stir-fry, are ideal to serve as a vegetarian main course. Others, such as Spinach with Straw Mushrooms, are best served as side dishes to complement the richer textures and more complex flavors of a main-course dish. Salads are also featured in this chapter, and, while most of these are best served as an accompaniment, some make delicious light lunches on their own.

MIXED VEGETABLES IN COCONUT MILK (PAGE 64)

VEGETABLE & NUT STIR-FRY

A colorful selection of vegetables are stir-fried in a creamy peanut sauce and sprinkled with nuts to serve.

SERVES 4

INGREDIENTS:

3 tbsp crunchy peanut butter
⅔ cup water
1 tbsp soy sauce
1 tsp sugar
1 carrot
¼ red onion
4 baby zucchini
1 red bell pepper, cored and
    deseeded
8 ounces egg thread noodles
¼ cup roughly chopped peanuts
2 tbsp vegetable oil
1 tsp sesame oil
1 small fresh green chili, deseeded and
    sliced thinly
1 garlic clove, sliced thinly
7½-ounce can water chestnuts, drained
    and sliced
3 cups bean sprouts
salt

1 ▼ Gradually blend the peanut butter with the water in a small bowl. Stir in the soy sauce and sugar.

2 Cut the carrot into thin matchsticks and slice the onion. Slice the zucchini on the diagonal and cut the bell pepper into chunks.

3 Bring a large pan of water to a boil and add the egg noodles. Remove from the heat immediately and let rest for 4 minutes, stirring occasionally to divide the noodles.

4 ▼ Heat a wok or large skillet, add the peanuts, and dry-fry until they are beginning to brown. Remove and set aside.

5 ▼ Add the vegetable and sesame oils to the wok or skillet and heat. Add the carrot, onion, zucchini, bell pepper, chili, and garlic, and stir-fry for 2–3 minutes. Add the water chestnuts, bean sprouts, and peanut sauce. Bring to a boil and heat thoroughly. Season to taste. Drain the noodles and serve with the stir-fried vegetables. Sprinkle with the peanuts.

CORN PATTIES

These little patties are very simple to prepare. They can be served as a light lunch or a first course, but also make a delicious addition to a party buffet. Serve them with a sweet chili sauce.

MAKES 12

INGREDIENTS:
11-ounce can corn kernels, drained
1 onion, chopped finely
1 tsp curry powder
1 garlic clove, crushed
1 tsp ground coriander
2 scallions, chopped
3 tbsp all-purpose flour
¼ tsp baking powder
salt
1 large egg
4 tbsp sunflower oil

1 ▲ Mash the drained corn kernels lightly in a medium-size bowl.

2 ▼ Then add all the remaining ingredients, except for the sunflower oil, one at a time and stirring after each addition.

3 ▼ Heat the sunflower oil in a large skillet. Drop large, rounded tablespoonfuls of the corn mixture carefully onto the hot oil, spacing them far enough apart so the corn patties do not to run into each other as they cook.

4 ▲ Cook for 4–5 minutes, turning each patty once, until they are golden brown and firm. Be careful not to turn them too soon, or they will break up.

5 Remove from the pan and drain on paper towels. Serve while still warm.

EGGPLANT IN CHILI SAUCE

Strips of eggplant are deep-fried in oil, then served in a fragrant chili sauce.

SERVES 4

❀❀❀❀❀❀❀❀❀❀❀❀❀❀❀❀❀❀❀

INGREDIENTS:
1 large eggplant
vegetable oil, for deep-frying
2 carrots
4 scallions
2 large garlic cloves
1 tbsp vegetable oil
2 tsp chili sauce
1 tbsp soy sauce
1 tbsp dry sherry

❀❀❀❀❀❀❀❀❀❀❀❀❀❀❀❀❀❀❀

1 ▼ Slice the eggplant crosswise, and then cut into strips about the size of french fries.

2 ▼ Heat enough oil in a heavy-based saucepan to deep-fry the eggplant in batches until just browned. The oil should be 350–375°F. Remove the fried eggplant strips with a perforated spoon and drain them on paper towels.

3 Cut the carrots into matchsticks. Trim and slice the scallions diagonally. Slice the garlic.

4 ▲ Heat 1 tablespoon of oil in a wok or large skillet. Add the carrot and stir-fry for 1 minute. Add the scallions and garlic, and stir-fry for another minute.

5 ▲ Stir in the chili sauce, soy sauce, and sherry, then stir in the drained fried eggplant. Mix well so the vegetables are heated through thoroughly before serving.

GREEN CURRY WITH TEMPEH

There are three basic curries in Thai cuisine, of which the green curry is the hottest. This green curry paste makes 6 tablespoons, enough for the recipe, and will keep for up to 3 weeks in the refrigerator. Serve over rice or noodles.

SERVES 4

INGREDIENTS:
1 tbsp sunflower oil
6 ounces marinated or plain tempeh or bean curd, cut into diamonds
6 scallions, cut into 1-inch pieces
⅔ cup coconut milk
Green Curry Paste (see below)
grated rind of 1 lime
¼ cup torn fresh basil leaves
¼ tsp liquid seasoning, such as Maggi

GREEN CURRY PASTE:
2 tsp coriander seeds
1 tsp cumin seeds
1 tsp black peppercorns
4 large fresh green chilies, deseeded
2 shallots, quartered
2 garlic cloves, peeled
2 tbsp chopped fresh cilantro, including root and stalk
grated rind of 1 lime
1 tbsp roughly chopped galangal
1 tsp ground turmeric
salt
2 tbsp oil

TO GARNISH:
fresh cilantro leaves
2 fresh green chilies, sliced thinly

1 To make the green curry paste, first grind together the coriander and cumin seeds with the peppercorns in a food processor or mortar and pestle.

2 Blend the remaining ingredients together and add the ground spice mixture. Store in a clean, dry jar for up to 3 weeks in the refrigerator, or freeze in a suitable container.

3 ▲ Heat the oil in a wok or large, heavy-based skillet. Add the tempeh and stir over a high heat for about 2 minutes until sealed on all sides. Add the scallions and stir-fry for 1 minute. Remove the tempeh and scallions and set aside.

4 Put half the coconut milk into the wok or skillet and bring to a boil. Add the curry paste and lime rind, and cook until fragrant, for about 1 minute. Add the reserved tempeh and scallions.

5 ▼ Add the remaining coconut milk and simmer for 7–8 minutes. Stir in the basil leaves and liquid seasoning. Simmer for another minute before serving, garnished with cilantro and chilies.

CHINESE HOT SALAD

A mixture of vegetables stir-fried with a Chinese flavor, with an added touch of chili. To serve cold, add 3–4 tablespoons of French dressing as the vegetables cool, then toss well and serve cold or chilled.

SERVES 4

INGREDIENTS:
1 tbsp dark soy sauce
1½–2 tsp sweet chili sauce
2 tbsp sherry
1 tbsp brown sugar
1 tbsp wine vinegar
2 tbsp sunflower oil
1 garlic clove, crushed
4 scallions, thinly sliced
   diagonally
8 ounces zucchini, cut into
   julienne strips about
   1½ inches long
8 ounces carrots, cut into
   julienne strips about
   1½ inches long
1 red or green bell pepper, cored,
   deseeded and thinly sliced
14-ounce can bean sprouts, well
   drained
4 ounces green beans, cut into
   2-inch lengths
1 tbsp sesame oil
salt and pepper
1–2 tsp sesame seeds, to garnish

1 ▼ Blend the soy sauce, chili sauce, sherry, sugar, vinegar, and seasonings together.

2 Heat the 2 tablespoons of sunflower oil in a wok or large skillet.

3 Add the garlic and scallions to the wok or skillet and stir-fry for 1–2 minutes.

4 ▲ Add the zucchini, carrots, and bell peppers, and stir-fry for 1–2 minutes. Add the soy sauce mixture and bring to a boil.

5 ▲ Add the bean sprouts and green beans and stir-fry for 1–2 minutes, making sure all the vegetables are thoroughly coated with the sauce.

6 Drizzle the sesame oil over the vegetables in the wok or skillet and stir-fry for about 30 seconds. Serve hot, sprinkled with sesame seeds.

GADO GADO SALAD

This salad is a mixture of cooked and raw vegetables served with a spicy peanut dressing.

SERVES 4

INGREDIENTS:
8 ounces new potatoes,
  scrubbed
1 cup trimmed green beans
1 cup small cauliflower florets
1¼ cups shredded white cabbage
1 carrot, cut into thin
  matchsticks
¼ cucumber, cut into chunks
2 cups fresh bean sprouts
2 hard-cooked eggs

SAUCE:
6 tbsp crunchy peanut butter
1¼ cups cold water
1 garlic clove, crushed
1 fresh red chili, deseeded and finely
  chopped
2 tbsp soy sauce
1 tbsp dry sherry
2 tsp sugar
1 tbsp lemon juice

1 Halve the potatoes and place in a saucepan of lightly salted water. Bring to a boil and then simmer for 12–15 minutes, or until cooked through. Drain and plunge into cold water.

2 ▼ Bring another pan of lightly salted water to a boil. Add the green beans, cauliflower, and cabbage, and cook for about 3 minutes. Drain and plunge into cold water.

3 ▼ Drain the vegetables. Arrange in piles on a large platter with the raw carrot, cucumber, and bean sprouts.

4 ▼ Shell the eggs, cut into quarters, and arrange on the salad. Cover and set aside.

5 ▲ To make the sauce, place the peanut butter in a bowl and blend in the water gradually, followed by the remaining ingredients.

6 Uncover the salad, place the sauce in a separate serving bowl, and drizzle some over each serving.

ORIENTAL SALAD

*This colorful, crisp salad has a fresh
orange dressing and is topped with
crunchy vermicelli.*

SERVES 4–6

INGREDIENTS:
¼ cup dried vermicelli
¼ head Chinese cabbage
2 cups bean sprouts
6 radishes
1 cup snow peas
1 large carrot
1 cup seed sprouts

DRESSING:
5 tbsp fresh orange juice
1 tbsp sesame seeds, toasted
1 tsp honey
1 tsp sesame oil
1 tbsp hazelnut oil

1 ▼ Break the vermicelli into small
strands. Heat a wok or large skillet
and dry-fry the vermicelli until lightly
golden. Remove from the wok or
skillet and set aside.

2 Shred the Chinese leaves and wash
with the bean sprouts. Drain
thoroughly and place in a large bowl.
Slice the radishes. Trim the snow peas
and cut each into 3 pieces. Cut the
carrot into thin matchsticks.

3 ▲ Add the seed sprouts and
prepared vegetables to the bowl.

4 Place all the dressing ingredients
in a screw-top jar and shake until
well-blended. Pour over the salad
and toss.

5 ▲ Transfer the salad to a serving
bowl and sprinkle over the reserved
vermicelli before serving.

CELERY & GREEN BELL PEPPER WITH SESAME DRESSING

This recipe makes a very elegant and light salad, which will complement rice and noodle dishes beautifully.

SERVES 4

INGREDIENTS:
2 cups bean sprouts
3 celery stalks, cut into
  1-inch pieces
1 large green bell pepper, chopped
1 large Granny Smith apple
2 tbsp sesame seeds,
  to garnish

DRESSING:
1½ tbsp chopped fresh cilantro
3 tbsp fresh lime juice
½ tsp mild chili powder
1 tsp sugar
½ tsp salt

1 Rinse and drain the bean sprouts. Pick them over and remove any that seem a little brown or limp – it is essential that they are fresh and crunchy for this recipe.

2 ▼ To make the dressing, combine the cilantro) lime juice, chili powder, sugar, and salt in a small bowl and mix thoroughly.

3 ▲ In a larger bowl, combine the celery, bell pepper, bean sprouts, and apple.

4 To prepare the garnish, toast the sesame seeds in a dry skillet until they are just turning color.

5 ▲ Stir the dressing into the mixed vegetables just before serving. Garnish with the toasted sesame seeds.

CARROT & CILANTRO SALAD

This is a tangy, crunchy salad, which is popular with everyone. It makes an ideal accompaniment to many oriental main-course dishes.

SERVES 4

❋❋❋❋❋❋❋❋❋❋❋❋❋❋❋❋

INGREDIENTS:
4 large carrots
2 celery stalks, cut into matchsticks
2 tbsp roughly chopped fresh
   cilantro

DRESSING:
1 tbsp sesame oil
1½ tbsp rice vinegar
½ tsp sugar
½ tsp salt

❋❋❋❋❋❋❋❋❋❋❋❋❋❋❋❋

1 ▼ To create flower-shaped carrot slices, as shown, cut several grooves lengthwise along each carrot before slicing it. Slice each carrot into very thin slices, using the slicing cutter of a grater.

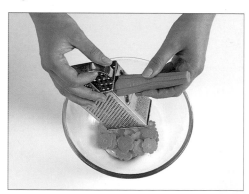

2 ▼ Combine the carrot, celery, and cilantro in a bowl.

3 ▲ To make the dressing, combine the sesame oil, rice vinegar, sugar, and salt in a separate bowl.

4 ▼ Just before serving, toss the carrot, celery, and cilantro mixture in the dressing and transfer to a serving dish.

THAI SALAD

This is a typical Thai-style salad made by mixing fruit and vegetables with the sharp, sweet, and fishy flavors of the dressing.

SERVES 4–6

INGREDIENTS:
2 cups finely shredded white cabbage
2 tomatoes, skinned, deseeded, and chopped
2 cups cooked green beans, halved
4 ounces peeled, cooked shrimp
1 papaya, peeled, deseeded, and chopped
1–2 fresh red chilies, deseeded and very finely sliced
scant ⅓ cup crushed roasted salted peanuts
handful of lettuce or baby spinach leaves, shredded or torn into small pieces

DRESSING:
4 tbsp lime juice
2 tbsp Thai fish sauce
sugar, to taste
pepper
sprigs of fresh cilantro, to garnish

1 ▼ Mix the cabbage with the chopped tomatoes, green beans, shrimp, three-quarters of the chopped papaya, and half the sliced chilies in a large bowl. Stir in two-thirds of the crushed roasted peanuts and mix thoroughly.

2 ▼ Line the rim of a large serving plate with the lettuce or spinach and pile the salad mixture into the center.

3 To make the dressing, beat the lime juice with the fish sauce. Add sugar and pepper to taste. Drizzle the dressing over the salad.

4 ▼ Scatter the top with the remaining papaya, chilies, and crushed peanuts. Garnish with fresh cilantro leaves and serve at once.

BRAISED CHINESE VEGETABLES

This dish is also known as Lo Han Zhai or Buddha's Delight. The original recipe calls for no less than 18 different vegetables to represent the 18 Buddhas (Lo Han).

SERVES 4

INGREDIENTS:
¼ ounce dried wood ears
1 cake bean curd
½ cup snow peas
4 ounces Chinese cabbage
1 small carrot
3 ounces canned baby corn, drained
3 ounces canned straw mushrooms, drained
2 ounces canned water chestnuts, drained
1¼ cups vegetable oil
1 tsp salt
½ tsp sugar
1 tbsp light soy sauce or oyster sauce
2–3 tbsp chicken stock or water
a few drops of sesame oil

1 Soak the wood ears in warm water for 15–20 minutes, then rinse and drain, discarding any hard bits, and dry on paper towels.

2 ▲ Cut the cake of bean curd into about 18 small pieces. Trim the snow peas. Cut the Chinese leaves and the carrot into slices that are roughly the same size and shape as the snow peas. Cut the baby corn, the straw mushrooms, and the water chestnuts in half.

3 ▼ Heat the oil in a preheated wok. Add the bean curd and deep-fry for about 2 minutes, until it turns slightly golden. Remove with a perforated spoon and drain on paper towels.

4 Pour off the oil, leaving about 2 tablespoons in the wok. Add the carrot, Chinese leaves, and snow peas. Stir-fry for about 1 minute.

5 ▲ Now add the baby corn, mushrooms, and water chestnuts. Stir gently for 2 more minutes, then add the salt, sugar, soy sauce, and stock or water. Bring to a boil and stir-fry for 1 more minute.

6 Sprinkle the vegetables with a few drops of sesame oil and serve hot or cold.

SPINACH WITH STRAW MUSHROOMS

Straw mushrooms are available in cans from oriental shops. Here they are served with spinach, raisins, and pine nuts. You can use button mushrooms instead, if straw mushrooms are unavailable.

SERVES 4

INGREDIENTS:
¼ cup pine nuts
1 pound fresh spinach leaves
3 tbsp vegetable oil
1 red onion, sliced
2 garlic cloves, sliced
14-ounce can straw mushrooms,
  drained
3 tbsp raisins
2 tbsp soy sauce
salt

1 ▼ Heat a wok or large heavy-based skillet and dry-fry the pine nuts until thc are lightly browned. Remove and set aside.

2 Wash the spinach thoroughly, picking the leaves over and removing long stalks. Drain and pat dry with paper towels.

3 ▲ Heat the oil in the wok or skillet. Add the onion and garlic, and stir-fry for 1 minute.

4 ▼ Add the spinach and straw mushrooms, and continue to stir-fry until the leaves have wilted. Drain off any excess liquid.

5 Stir in the raisins, reserved pine nuts, and soy sauce. Stir-fry until heated completely through and well-mixed. Season to taste with salt before serving.

STIR-FRIED BEAN SPROUTS

Be sure to use fresh bean sprouts, rather than the canned variety, for this crunchy-textured dish.

SERVES 4

❁❁❁❁❁❁❁❁❁❁❁❁❁❁

INGREDIENTS:
4 cups fresh bean sprouts
2–3 scallions
1 medium fresh red chili (optional)
3 tbsp vegetable oil
¼ tsp salt
¼ tsp sugar
1 tbsp light soy sauce
few drops of sesame oil (optional)

❁❁❁❁❁❁❁❁❁❁❁❁❁❁

1 ▼ Rinse the bean sprouts in cold water, discarding any husks or small pieces that float to the top. Drain well on paper towels.

2 ▼ Trim the scallions and cut them into short sections. Thinly shred the fresh red chili, if using, discarding the seeds.

3 ▲ Heat the oil in a preheated wok. Add the bean sprouts, scallions, and shredded chili, if using, and stir-fry for about 2 minutes.

4 ▼ Add the salt, sugar, soy sauce, and sesame oil, if using, to the mixture in the wok. Stir well to blend. Serve hot or cold.

GOLDEN NEEDLES WITH BAMBOO SHOOTS

Golden needles are the dried flower buds of the tiger lily. They are usually sold in the dried form and can be obtained from oriental food markets. They give a unique musky flavor to this dish.

SERVES 4

INGREDIENTS:
¼ cup dried lily flowers
2 x 7¼-ounce cans bamboo shoots, drained
¼ cup cornstarch
vegetable oil, for deep-frying
1 tbsp vegetable oil
scant 2 cups vegetable stock
1 tbsp dark soy sauce
1 tbsp dry sherry
1 tsp sugar
1 large garlic clove, sliced
¼ each red, green, and yellow bell peppers

1 ▼ Soak the lily flowers in hot water for 30 minutes.

2 Coat the bamboo shoots in cornstarch. Heat enough oil in a large heavy-based saucepan to deep-fry the bamboo shoots in batches until they are just beginning to color. The oil should be 350–375°F, or hot enough so a bread cube browns in 30 seconds. Remove the bamboo shoots with a perforated spoon and drain them on paper towels.

3 ▼ Drain the lily flowers and trim off the hard ends. Heat 1 tablespoon of vegetable oil in a wok or large skillet. Add the lily flowers, bamboo shoots, vegetable stock, soy sauce, sherry, sugar, and garlic.

4 ▼ Slice the colored bell peppers thinly and add to the wok or skillet. Bring to a boil, stirring constantly, then reduce the heat and simmer for 5 minutes. Add extra water or stock, if necessary.

BROCCOLI IN OYSTER SAUCE

Some Cantonese restaurants use only the stalks of the broccoli for this dish, for added crunch. If the stalks are cut very thinly, they can be added to the pan at the same time as the florets.

SERVES 4

INGREDIENTS:
8–10 ounces broccoli
3 tbsp vegetable oil
3–4 small slices fresh ginger
¼ tsp salt
¼ tsp sugar
3–4 tbsp chicken stock or water
1 tbsp oyster sauce

1 ▼ Cut the broccoli spears into small florets. Trim the stalks, peel off the rough skin, and cut the stalks diagonally into diamond shapes.

2 ▼ Heat the oil in a preheated wok and add the pieces of stalk and the ginger. Stir-fry for 30 seconds, then add the florets and continue to stir-fry for another 2 minutes.

3 ▲ Add the salt, sugar, and stock or water, and continue stirring for another minute or so.

4 ▼ Blend in the oyster sauce, stirring to coat the broccoli well. Serve hot or cold.

SWEET & SOUR VEGETABLES

Make your own choice of vegetables from the suggested list, but be sure to include scallions and garlic. For a hotter, spicier sauce, add bottled chili sauce.

SERVES 4

INGREDIENTS:

5–6 vegetables from the following:
1 red, green, or yellow bell pepper, cored, deseeded, and sliced
1 cup trimmed green beans, cut into 2–3 pieces
1 cup trimmed snow peas, cut into 2–3 pieces each
2 cups small broccoli or cauliflower florets
2 cups zucchini, cut into thin 2-inch lengths
1¼ cups carrots, cut into julienne strips
1 cup thinly sliced baby corn
2 leeks, sliced thinly and cut into matchsticks
1¼ cups finely diced parsnip
1¼ cups finely diced celery root
3 celery stalks, thinly sliced crosswise
4 tomatoes, skinned, quartered, and deseeded
1¼ cups thinly sliced button or closed-cup mushrooms
3-inch piece cucumber, diced
7-ounce can water chestnuts or bamboo shoots, drained and sliced
15-ounce can bean sprouts or hearts of palm, drained and sliced
4 scallions, trimmed and thinly sliced
1 garlic clove, crushed
2 tbsp sunflower oil

SWEET & SOUR SAUCE:

2 tbsp wine vinegar
2 tbsp clear honey
1 tbsp tomato paste
2 tbsp soy sauce
2 tbsp sherry
1–2 tsp sweet chili sauce (optional)
2 tsp cornstarch

1 ▲ Prepare the selected vegetables, cutting them into uniform lengths.

2 ▼ Combine the sauce ingredients in a bowl, blending well together.

3 Heat the oil in the wok, swirling it around until it is really hot. Add the scallions and garlic, and stir-fry for 1 minute.

4 ▼ Add the prepared vegetables – the harder ones first – and stir-fry for 2 minutes. Then add the softer mushrooms, snow peas, and tomatoes, and stir-fry for 2 minutes.

5 ▼ Add the sauce and bring to a boil quickly, tossing all the vegetables until they are thoroughly coated and the sauce has thickened. Serve hot.

MIXED VEGETABLES IN COCONUT MILK

This is a deliciously crunchy way to prepare a mixture of vegetables.

SERVES 4–6

INGREDIENTS:
*1 fresh red chili, deseeded
  and chopped
1 tsp coriander seeds
1 tsp cumin seeds
2 garlic cloves, crushed
1¼ tbsp lime juice
1 cup coconut milk
2 cups fresh bean sprouts
2 cups shredded white cabbage
1 cup trimmed snow peas
1¼ cups thinly sliced carrots
1¼ cups cauliflower florets
3 tbsp peanut butter
grated or shaved coconut,
  to garnish*

1 Grind together the chili, coriander and cumin seeds, garlic, and lime juice in a mortar and pestle, spice grinder, or food processor.

2 ▼ Put the spices into a medium saucepan and heat gently until fragrant, about 1 minute. Add the coconut milk and stir until just about to boil.

3 ▼ Meanwhile, mix all the prepared vegetables together in a large bowl.

4 ▲ Stir the peanut butter into the coconut mixture and combine with the vegetables. Sprinkle over the grated or shaved coconut and serve immediately.

MEAT & POULTRY DISHES

Included in this chapter is a delectable range of chicken, duck, beef, and pork dishes, from familiar oriental favorites like Lemon Chicken and Aromatic & Crispy Duck, through Japanese-inspired sukiyaki and teriyaki dishes, to Thai green curries. Some of the dishes, such as the Thai-flavored Roast Baby Chickens, are adapted slightly for Westerners, but have all the exotic flavors of the Orient. You will find many different cooking techniques used throughout this chapter. Beef can be cooked by various methods, and one of the favorites is stir-frying, which gives the meat a slightly dry, chewy texture. Braising and steaming are popular Szechuan methods of cooking beef and pork, and this method results in tender meat. Double-cooking also results in succulent meat; in this method the meat is first tenderized by a long, slow simmering in water, followed by a quick crisping or stir-frying in a sauce – Twice-Cooked Pork is a delicious example of this technique.

SUKIYAKI BEEF

An easy way of giving beef a Japanese flavor is to marinate the meat in teriyaki sauce and sherry: it can be left for anything from 1–24 hours. Hearts of palm and mushrooms blend well with the beef.

SERVES 4

INGREDIENTS:
1-inch piece fresh ginger, grated
1 garlic clove, crushed
4 tbsp sherry
4 tbsp teriyaki sauce
*1–1¼ pounds sirloin, rump, or
    fillet steak*
15-ounce can hearts of palm
2 tbsp sesame or sunflower oil
*1 cup thinly sliced button or closed-cup
    mushrooms*
salt and pepper

TO GARNISH:
sesame seeds (optional)
scallion tassels

1 Blend the ginger in a shallow dish with the garlic, sherry, and teriyaki sauce, adding a little salt.

2 ▼ Cut the steak into narrow strips, about 1–1¼ inches long, across the grain. Add the strips to the marinade in the dish, mix to coat, cover, and let marinate in the refrigerator for at least 1 hour and up to 24 hours.

3 Drain the hearts of palm and cut into slanting slices, about ½ inch thick.

4 ▼ Remove the beef from the marinade with a perforated spoon, reserving the marinade. Heat the oil in the wok, swirling it around until it is really hot. Add the beef and stir-fry for 2 minutes, then add the mushrooms and continue to cook for another minute.

5 ▲ Add the hearts of palm to the wok with the reserved marinade and stir-fry for another minute, making sure the meat is thoroughly coated in the sauce. Taste and adjust the seasoning. Serve sprinkled with sesame seeds, if using, and garnished with scallion tassels.

BEEF WITH BEANS

Strips of steak with a strong flavoring of sherry, teriyaki sauce, and orange make this an ideal dish for entertaining.

SERVES 4

INGREDIENTS:
1–1¼ pounds sirloin, rump, or fillet
  steak
1 orange
2 tbsp sesame oil
4 scallions, thinly sliced
  diagonally
1¼ cups trimmed green beans, cut
  into 2–3 pieces each
1 garlic clove, crushed
4 tbsp sherry
1½ tbsp teriyaki sauce
¼ tsp ground allspice
1 tsp sugar
15-ounce can cannellini beans,
  drained
salt and pepper

TO GARNISH:
orange slices
fresh bay leaves

1 Cut the steak into narrow strips, about 1½ inches long, cutting across the grain.

2 ▲ Remove the rind from the orange using a citrus zester or stripper, or pare thinly with a vegetable peeler, and cut the rind into julienne strips. Squeeze the orange and reserve the juice.

3 ▲ Heat 1 tablespoon of the oil in a wok or large skillet. Add the strips of beef and stir-fry briskly for about 2 minutes, then remove from the wok and keep warm.

4 Add the remaining oil. When hot, add the scallions and garlic, and stir-fry for 1–2 minutes. Add the green beans and continue to cook for 2 minutes.

5 ▼ Add the sherry, teriyaki, orange rind and 3 tablespoons of orange juice, allspice, sugar, and seasoning. When well mixed, return the beef and any juices to the wok.

6 Stir-fry for 1–2 minutes, then add the cannellini beans and stir until piping hot. Adjust the seasoning. Serve garnished with orange slices and bay leaves.

BEEF & BOK CHOY

A colorful selection of vegetables are stir-fried with tender strips of steak.

SERVES 4

✿✿✿✿✿✿✿✿✿✿✿✿✿✿✿✿✿

INGREDIENTS:
*1 large head of bok choy, about
    8–9 ounces, roughly torn
2 tbsp vegetable oil
2 garlic cloves, crushed
1 pound rump or fillet steak, cut
    into thin strips
1¼ cups trimmed snow peas
1¼ cups baby corn, sliced
    if large
6 scallions, chopped
2 red bell peppers, cored, deseeded,
    and thinly sliced
2 tbsp oyster sauce
1 tbsp Thai fish sauce
1 tbsp sugar*

✿✿✿✿✿✿✿✿✿✿✿✿✿✿✿✿✿

1 ▼ Steam the bok choy leaves over boiling water until just tender. Keep warm.

2 ▼ Heat the oil in a large, heavy-based skillet or wok, add the

garlic and beef strips, and stir-fry until just browned, for about 1–2 minutes.

3 ▲ Add the trimmed snow peas, baby corn, chopped scallions, sliced red bell pepper, oyster sauce, Thai fish sauce, and sugar to the skillet or wok.

4 ▼ Mix well and stir-fry for another 2–3 minutes, until the vegetables are just tender but still crisp.

5 Arrange the bok choy leaves in the base of a heated serving dish. Spoon the beef and vegetable mixture into the center. Serve immediately, with rice or noodles.

BEEF & CHILI BLACK BEAN SAUCE

It is not necessary to use the expensive cuts of steak for this recipe. Because the meat is cut into small, thin slices and marinated, it will be tender.

SERVES 4

INGREDIENTS:
*8–10 ounces steak, such as rump
1 small onion
1 small green bell pepper, cored
    and deseeded
about 1¼ cups vegetable oil
1 scallion, trimmed and cut into short
    sections
few small slices of fresh ginger
1–2 small fresh green or red chilies,
    deseeded and sliced
2 tbsp black bean sauce,
    crushed*

MARINADE:
*¼ tsp baking soda or
    baking powder
¼ tsp sugar
1 tbsp light soy sauce
2 tsp Chinese rice wine
    or dry sherry
2 tsp cornstarch paste
    (see page 15)
2 tsp sesame oil*

1 ▼ Cut the steak into thin strips. Mix the marinade ingredients together in a shallow dish, add the steak strips, turn to coat, and let marinate for at least 2–3 hours – the longer the better.

2 Cut the onion and green bell pepper into small cubes.

3 ▼ Heat the vegetable oil in a preheated wok or a large skillet. Add the marinated steak strips and stir-fry for about 1 minute, or until the color changes. Remove the strips from the oil with a perforated spoon and drain on paper towels. Keep warm.

4 ▲ Pour off the excess oil, leaving about 1 tablespoon in the wok or skillet. Add the scallion, ginger, chilies, onion, and green bell pepper, and stir-fry for about 1 minute. Add the black bean sauce, stir until smooth, then return the steak strips to the wok or skillet. Blend well and stir-fry for another minute. Serve hot.

GREEN CHILI CHICKEN

The green chili paste gives a hot and spicy flavor to the chicken, which takes on a vibrant green color.

SERVES 4

INGREDIENTS:
5 tbsp vegetable oil
1 pound boneless chicken breasts, sliced
  into thin strips
¼ cup coconut milk
3 tbsp brown sugar
3 tsp Thai fish sauce
3 tbsp sliced fresh red and green chilies,
  deseeded
4–6 tbsp chopped fresh basil
3 tbsp thick coconut milk or cream
finely chopped fresh chilies and lemon
  grass, and lemon slices,
  to garnish

GREEN CURRY PASTE:
2 tsp ground ginger
2 tsp ground coriander
2 tsp caraway seeds,
2 tsp ground nutmeg
2 tsp shrimp paste
2 tsp salt
2 tsp black pepper
pinch of ground cloves
1 lemon grass stalk, finely chopped
2 tbsp chopped cilantro
2 garlic cloves, peeled
2 onions, peeled
grated rind and juice of 2 limes
4 fresh green chilies, each about
  2 inches long, deseeded

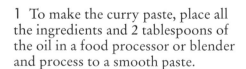

1 To make the curry paste, place all the ingredients and 2 tablespoons of the oil in a food processor or blender and process to a smooth paste.

2 Heat the remaining oil in a heavy-based skillet or wok. Add the curry paste and cook for about 30 seconds.

3 ▼ Add the chicken strips to the wok or skillet and stir-fry over a high heat for about 2–3 minutes.

4 Add the coconut milk, brown sugar, fish sauce, and chilies. Cook for 5 minutes, stirring frequently.

5 ▲ Remove from the heat, add the basil, and toss well to mix.

6 Transfer the chicken to a warmed serving dish. To serve, spoon on a little of the thick coconut milk or cream and garnish with chopped chilies, lemon grass, and lemon slices. Serve with steamed or boiled rice.

PEPPERED BEEF CASHEWS

A simple but stunning dish of tender strips of beef mixed with crunchy cashews, coated in a hot sauce. Serve with rice noodles.

SERVES 6

INGREDIENTS:
1 tbsp peanut or sunflower oil
1 tbsp sesame oil
1 onion, sliced
1 garlic clove, crushed
1 tbsp grated fresh ginger
1 pound fillet or rump steak, cut into thin strips
2 tsp palm or brown crystal sugar
2 tbsp light soy sauce
1 small yellow bell pepper, cored, deseeded, and sliced
1 red bell pepper, cored, deseeded, and sliced
4 scallions, chopped
2 celery stalks, chopped
4 large open-cap mushrooms, sliced
4 tbsp roasted cashews
3 tbsp stock or white wine

2 ▲ Add the steak strips and stir-fry for another 2–3 minutes, until the meat has browned. Add the sugar and soy sauce, mixing well.

3 Add the bell peppers, scallions, celery, mushrooms, and cashews, mixing well.

4 ▼ Add the stock or wine and stir-fry for 2–3 minutes, until the meat is cooked through and the vegetables are tender-crisp.

5 Serve the stir-fry immediately with rice noodles.

1 Heat the oils in a wok or a large, heavy-based skillet. Add the onion, garlic, and ginger. Stir-fry for about 2 minutes, until softened and lightly colored.

LEMON CHICKEN

Lemon sauce is a easily available from oriental stores, or you can make your own. It is a Cantonese speciality.

SERVES 4

INGREDIENTS:

*12 ounces chicken breast fillets,
  skinned
1 tbsp Chinese rice wine or dry sherry
1 egg, beaten
4 tbsp all-purpose flour, blended with
  2 tbsp water
vegetable oil, for deep-frying
Lemon Sauce (see below), or
  a bottled commercial variety
salt and pepper
slices of fresh lemon, to garnish
plain boiled rice, to serve (optional)*

LEMON SAUCE:

*1 tbsp vegetable oil
1 cup chicken stock
1 tbsp superfine sugar
1 tbsp lemon juice
1 tbsp cornstarch
1 tsp salt
1 tsp grated lemon rind*

1 To make the lemon sauce, heat the oil in a wok or saucepan until hot, reduce the heat, and add all the other sauce ingredients. Blend well, then bring to a boil and stir until smooth.

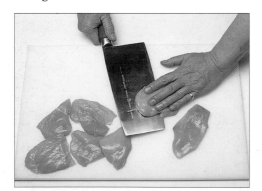

2 ▲ Cut the chicken into thin slices and place in a shallow dish with the wine, salt, and pepper. Let marinate for 25–30 minutes.

3 Make a batter by mixing together the beaten egg and the flour paste. Place the chicken slices in the batter and turn to coat well.

4 ▲ Heat the oil in a wok or deep-fat fryer to 350–375°F, or until a cube of bread browns in 30 seconds when dropped into the hot oil. Deep-fry the chicken slices until golden brown,

then remove with a perforated spoon and drain on paper towels. Cut the chicken slices into bite-size pieces.

5 ▼ Heat about 1 tablespoon of oil in a wok or pan. Stir in the prepared lemon sauce until well blended, and then pour evenly over the chicken. Garnish with lemon slices and serve with rice, if wished.

PEANUT SESAME CHICKEN

In this quickly prepared dish, chicken strips are stir-fried with vegetables. Sesame and peanuts give extra crunch and flavor, and the fruit juice glaze gives a lovely shiny coating to the sauce.

SERVES 4

INGREDIENTS:

2 tbsp vegetable oil
2 tbsp sesame oil
1 pound boneless, skinned
   chicken breasts, sliced
   into strips
2 cups small broccoli florets
2 cups baby corn, halved
   if large
1 small red bell pepper, cored,
   deseeded, and sliced
2 tbsp soy sauce
1 cup orange juice
2 tsp cornstarch
2 tbsp toasted sesame seeds
⅓ cup roasted, shelled, unsalted
   peanuts
rice or noodles, to serve

1 Heat the oils in a wok or large, heavy-based skillet, add the chicken strips, and stir-fry until browned, for about 4–5 minutes.

2 ▲ Add the broccoli, corn, and red bell pepper. Stir-fry for another 1–2 minutes.

3 ▼ Meanwhile, mix the soy sauce with the orange juice and cornstarch. Stir into the chicken and vegetable mixture, stirring constantly until the sauce has slightly thickened and a glaze develops.

4 ▼ Stir in the toasted sesame seeds and roasted peanuts, mixing well. Heat for another 3–4 minutes. Serve immediately, with rice or noodles.

CHICKEN WITH BEAN SPROUTS

This is the basic chicken chop suey that is found in almost every Chinese restaurant in the world.

SERVES 4

✻✻✻✻✻✻✻✻✻✻✻✻✻✻✻

INGREDIENTS:
4 ounces chicken breast fillet,
* skinned*
1 tsp salt
¼ egg white, lightly beaten
2 tsp cornstarch paste
* (see page 15)*
about 1⅔ cups vegetable oil
1 small onion, thinly shredded
1 small green bell pepper, cored,
* deseeded, and thinly shredded*
1 small carrot, thinly shredded
2 cups fresh bean sprouts
¼ tsp sugar
1 tbsp light soy sauce
1 tsp Chinese rice wine or dry sherry
2–3 tbsp Chinese Stock
* (see page 10)*
few drops of sesame oil
chili sauce, to serve

✻✻✻✻✻✻✻✻✻✻✻✻✻✻✻

1 Thinly shred the chicken and mix with a pinch of the salt, the egg white, and cornstarch paste.

2 ▲ Heat the oil in a preheated wok or large skillet, and stir-fry the chicken for about 1 minute, stirring to separate the shreds. Remove with a perforated spoon and drain on paper towels.

3 ▼ Pour off the oil, leaving about 2 tablespoons in the wok or skillet. Add all the vegetables, except the bean sprouts, and stir-fry for about 2 minutes. Add the bean sprouts and stir for a few more seconds.

4 ▲ Add the chicken with the remaining salt, sugar, soy sauce, and wine. Blend well and add the stock or water. Sprinkle with the sesame oil and serve at once, accompanied by the chili sauce.

KUNG PO CHICKEN WITH CASHEWS

Peanuts, walnuts, or almonds can be used instead of the cashews, if preferred.

SERVES 4

❀❀❀❀❀❀❀❀❀❀❀❀❀❀❀❀❀

INGREDIENTS:

8–10 ounces chicken meat, boned and skinned
¼ tsp salt
¼ egg white
1 tsp cornstarch paste (see page 15)
1 medium green bell pepper, cored and deseeded
4 tbsp vegetable oil
1 scallion, trimmed and cut into short sections
few small slices of fresh ginger
4–5 small dried red chilies, soaked, deseeded, and shredded
2 tbsp crushed yellow bean sauce
1 tsp Chinese rice wine or dry sherry
4 ounces roasted cashews
few drops of sesame oil
plain boiled rice, to serve

❀❀❀❀❀❀❀❀❀❀❀❀❀❀❀❀❀

1 ▼ Cut the chicken into small cubes, about the size of sugar lumps. Place the chicken in a small bowl and mix with a pinch of salt, the egg white, and then the cornstarch paste, in that order.

2 Cut the green bell pepper into cubes or triangles, about the same size as the chicken pieces.

3 ▼ Heat the oil in a preheated wok or skillet, add the chicken cubes, and stir-fry for about 1 minute, or until the color changes. Remove with a perforated spoon and keep warm.

4 Add the scallion, ginger, chilies, and green bell pepper. Stir-fry for about 1 minute.

5 ▼ Add the chicken with the yellow bean sauce and wine. Blend well and stir-fry for another minute. Finally stir in the cashews and sesame oil. Serve hot with rice.

ROAST BABY CHICKENS

Baby chickens, stuffed with lemon grass and lime leaves, coated with a spicy Thai paste, then roasted until crisp and golden, make a wonderful, aromatic dish for a special occasion.

SERVES 4

INGREDIENTS:
4 small baby chickens, weighing about
  12 ounces–1 pound each
mixed wild and basmati rice, to serve

TO GARNISH:
fresh cilantro leaves
lime wedges

MARINADE:
4 garlic cloves, peeled
2 fresh cilantro roots
1 tbsp light soy sauce
salt and pepper

STUFFING:
4 lemon grass stalks
4 kaffir lime leaves
4 slices fresh ginger
about 6 tbsp coconut milk, to brush

1 Wash the chickens and pat dry with paper towels.

2 ▲ Place all the ingredients for the marinade in a blender and process until smooth, or grind down in a pestle and mortar. Season to taste with salt and pepper. Rub the marinade mixture into the skin of the chickens, using the back of a spoon to spread it evenly over the skins.

3 Place a stalk of lemon grass, a lime leaf, and a piece of ginger in the cavity of each chicken.

4 ▼ Place the stuffed chickens in a large roasting pan and brush lightly with the coconut milk. Roast for 30 minutes in a preheated oven at 400°F.

5 Remove from the oven and brush again with coconut milk.

6 ▼ Return the chicken to the oven and cook for another 15–25 minutes, until golden and cooked through, depending on the size of the chickens. The chickens are cooked when the juices from the thigh run clear when pricked with a sharp knife and are not tinged pink.

7 Serve with the pan juices poured over the chicken. Garnish with cilantro leaves and lime wedges.

AROMATIC & CRISPY DUCK

Although the pancakes traditionally served with this dish are not too difficult to make, the process is very time-consuming. Buy ready-made ones from oriental stores, or use crisp lettuce leaves as the wrapper.

SERVES 4

INGREDIENTS:
2 large duckling quarters
1 tsp salt
3–4 pieces star anise
1 tsp Szechuan red peppercorns
1 tsp cloves
2 cinnamon sticks, broken
    into pieces
2–3 scallions, trimmed and cut into
    short sections
4–5 small slices fresh ginger
3–4 tbsp Chinese rice wine or
    dry sherry
vegetable oil, for deep-frying

TO SERVE:
12 purchased oriental pancakes, or
    12 crisp lettuce leaves
hoisin or plum sauce
⅓ cucumber, thinly shredded
3–4 scallions, thinly shredded

1 ▲ Place the duck pieces in a shallow glass dish and rub with the salt. Arrange the star anise, peppercorns, cloves, and cinnamon on top. Sprinkle with the scallions, ginger, and rice wine or sherry, and let marinate for at least 3–4 hours.

2 ▼ Arrange the duck pieces (with the marinade spices) on a plate that will fit inside a bamboo steamer. Pour some hot water into a wok, place the bamboo steamer in the wok, on a rack or trivet. Put in the duck and cover with the bamboo lid. Steam the duck pieces (with the marinade) over a high heat for at least 2–3 hours, until tender and cooked through. Refill the hot water from time to time, as needed.

3 Remove the duck and let cool for at least 4–5 hours – this is very important; unless the duck is cold and dry, it will not be crispy.

4 ▲ Pour off the water and wipe the wok dry. Pour in the oil and heat until smoking. Deep-fry the duck pieces, skin-side down, for 4–5 minutes, or until crisp and brown. Remove and drain on paper towels.

5 To serve, scrape the meat off the bone, place about 1 teaspoon of hoisin or plum sauce on the center of a pancake or lettuce leaf, add a few pieces of cucumber and scallion with a portion of the duck meat. Wrap up to form a small parckage and eat with your fingers. Provide plenty of paper napkins for your guests.

DUCK WITH GINGER & LIME

*Just the thing for a lazy summer day –
roasted duck breasts sliced and served
with a dressing made of ginger, lime
juice, sesame oil, and fish sauce. Serve
on a bed of assorted fresh salad leaves.*

SERVES 6

INGREDIENTS:
*3 boneless duck breasts, about
    8 ounces each
salt*

DRESSING:
*¼ cup olive oil
2 tsp sesame oil
2 tbsp lime juice
grated rind and juice of 1 orange
2 tsp Thai fish sauce
1 tbsp grated fresh ginger
1 garlic clove, crushed
2 tsp light soy sauce
3 scallions, finely chopped
1 tsp sugar
about 8 ounces assorted salad leaves
orange slices, to garnish
    (optional)*

1 ▼ Wash the duck breasts, dry on
paper towels, then cut in half. Prick
the skin all over with a fork and
season well with salt.

2 Place the duck pieces, skin-side
down, on a wire rack or trivet over a
roasting pan. Cook the duck in a
preheated oven at 400°F for
10 minutes.

3 Turn over and cook for another
12–15 minutes, or until the duck is
cooked, but still pink in the center,
and the skin is crisp.

4 ▼ To make the dressing, beat the
oils with the lime juice, orange rind
and juice, fish sauce, ginger, garlic,
soy sauce, scallions, and sugar, until
well blended.

5 ▼ Remove the duck from the oven,
let cool, then cut into thick slices. Add
a little of the dressing to moisten and
coat the duck.

6 To serve, arrange salad leaves on a
serving dish. Top with the sliced duck
breasts and drizzle with the remaining
salad dressing. Garnish with orange
slices, if using, and serve at once.

DUCK WITH PINEAPPLE

For best results, use the cooked duck available from Chinese restaurants. Red wine vinegar can be substituted for the rice vinegar in the recipe.

SERVES 4

INGREDIENTS:
4–6 ounces cooked duck meat
3 tbsp vegetable oil
1 small onion, thinly shredded
2–3 slices fresh ginger, thinly shredded
1 scallion, thinly shredded
1 small carrot, thinly shredded
4 ounces canned pineapple, cut into
   small slices
¼ tsp salt
1 tbsp red rice vinegar
2 tbsp syrup from the pineapple
1 tbsp cornstarch paste
   (see page 15)
black bean sauce, to serve (optional)

1 ▲ Cut the cooked duck into strips.

2 ▼ Heat the oil in a preheated wok, add the shredded onion, and stir-fry until opaque.

3 Add the shredded ginger, scallion, and carrot. Stir-fry for about 1 minute.

4 ▲ Add the duck and pineapple, with the salt, vinegar, and pineapple syrup. Stir until well blended.

5 ▼ Add the cornstarch paste and stir for 1–2 minutes, until the sauce has thickened. Serve hot with the black bean sauce, if using.

SPARE RIBS WITH CHILI

For best results, chop the spare ribs into small bite-size pieces.

SERVES 4

INGREDIENTS:

1 pound pork spare ribs
1 tsp sugar
1 tbsp light soy sauce
1 tsp Chinese rice wine or
dry sherry
1 tsp cornstarch
about 2¼ cups vegetable oil
1 garlic clove, finely chopped
1 scallion, cut into short pieces
1 small fresh red or green chili, thinly
sliced
2 tbsp black bean sauce
about ⅔ cup Chinese Stock (see page 10)
or water
1 small onion, diced
1 medium green bell pepper, cored,
deseeded, and diced

1 ▲ Trim excess fat from the ribs and chop each rib into 3–4 bite-size pieces. Place the ribs in a shallow dish with the sugar, soy sauce, rice wine, and cornstarch. Let marinate for 35–45 minutes.

2 ▼ Heat the oil in a preheated wok until a bread cube browns in 30 seconds. Add the spare ribs and deep-fry for 2–3 minutes, until light brown. Remove with a perforated spoon and drain on paper towels.

3 Pour off the oil, leaving 1 tablespoon in the wok. Add the garlic, scallion, chili, and black bean sauce, and stir-fry for 30–40 seconds.

4 Add the spare ribs, blend well, then add the stock or water. Bring to a boil, then reduce the heat, cover, and braise for 8–10 minutes, stirring once or twice.

5 ▼ Add the onion and green bell pepper to the wok, increase the heat to high, and stir uncovered for about 2 minutes to reduce the sauce a little. Serve hot.

SWEET & SOUR PORK RIBS

Spare ribs, the traditional Chinese-style rib, have been used here. Baby back and loin ribs are also suitable.

SERVES 4–6

❋❋❋❋❋❋❋❋❋❋❋❋❋❋❋❋

INGREDIENTS:
2 garlic cloves, crushed
2-inch piece fresh ginger, peeled and grated
⅔ cup soy sauce
2 tbsp sugar
4 tbsp sweet sherry
4 tbsp tomato paste
2 cups cubed pineapple
4 pounds pork spare ribs
3 tbsp clear honey
5 pineapple rings, fresh or canned

❋❋❋❋❋❋❋❋❋❋❋❋❋❋❋❋

1 ▼ Combine the garlic, ginger, soy sauce, sugar, sherry, tomato paste, and cubed pineapple in a nonporous dish.

2 ▼ Put the spare ribs into the dish and make sure that they are coated completely with the marinade. Cover the dish.

3 Leave at room temperature for 2 hours only.

4 ▲ Cook the ribs on a medium-hot outdoor grill for 30–40 minutes, brushing with the honey after 20–30 minutes. Baste frequently with the reserved marinade, until cooked.

5 ▲ Cook the pineapple rings on the grill for about 10 minutes, turning once.

6 Serve the ribs with the charred pineapple rings on the side.

TWICE-COOKED PORK

Twice-cooked is a popular way of cooking meat in China. The meat is first boiled to tenderize it, then cut into strips or slices and stir-fried.

SERVES 4

INGREDIENTS:

8–10 ounces shoulder or leg of pork, in one piece
1 small green bell pepper, cored and deseeded
1 small red bell pepper, cored and deseeded
4 ounces canned sliced bamboo shoots, rinsed and drained
3 tbsp vegetable oil
1 scallion, cut into short pieces
1 tsp salt
¼ tsp sugar
1 tbsp light soy sauce
1 tsp chili bean sauce or finely chopped fresh chili
1 tsp Chinese rice wine or dry sherry
few drops of sesame oil

1 ▲ Immerse the pork in a saucepan of boiling water to cover. Return to a boil and skim the surface. Reduce the heat, cover, and simmer for 15–20 minutes. Turn off the heat and leave the pork in the water to cool for at least 2–3 hours.

2 ▼ Remove the pork from the water and drain well. Trim off any excess fat, then cut into small, thin slices. Cut the green and red bell peppers into pieces, about the same size as the pork and the sliced bamboo shoots.

3 Heat the oil in a preheated wok or skillet, and add the vegetables and scallion. Stir-fry for about 1 minute.

4 ▼ Add the pork, followed by the salt, sugar, soy sauce, chili bean sauce, and rice wine or sherry. Blend well, continue stirring for another minute, then sprinkle with a few drops of sesame oil and serve.

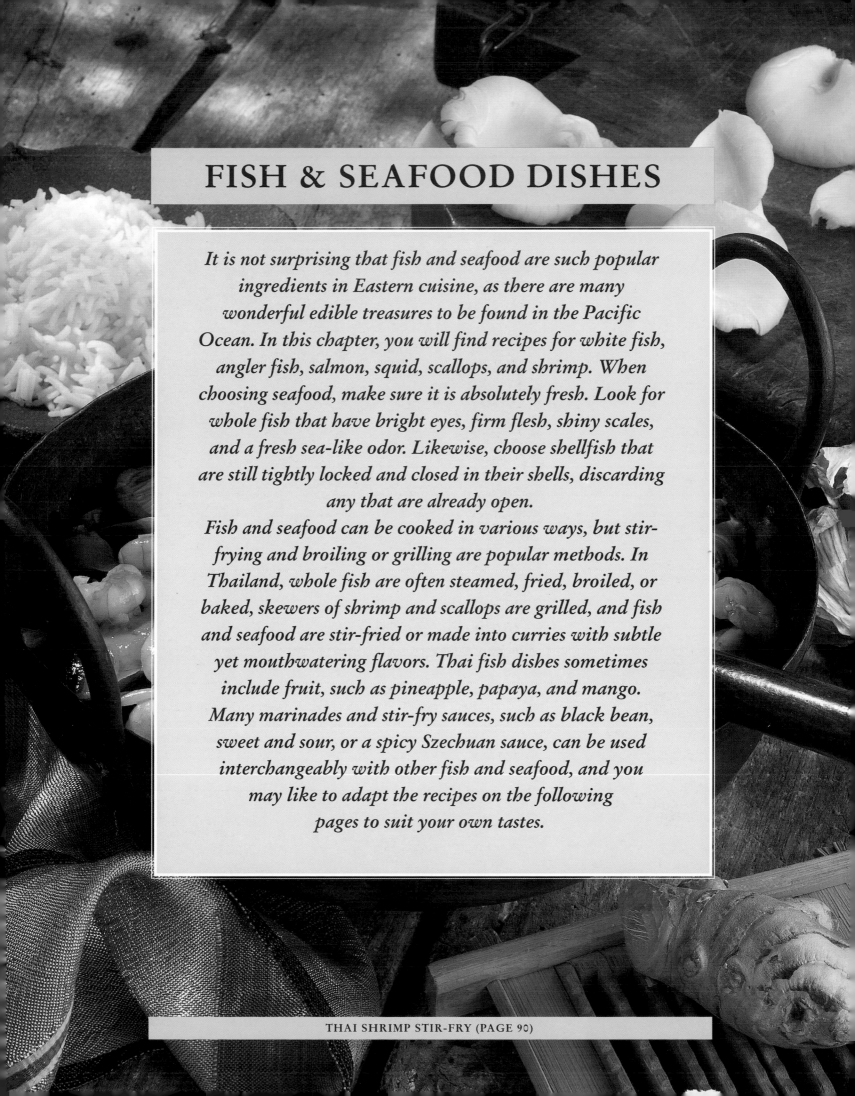

FISH & SEAFOOD DISHES

It is not surprising that fish and seafood are such popular ingredients in Eastern cuisine, as there are many wonderful edible treasures to be found in the Pacific Ocean. In this chapter, you will find recipes for white fish, angler fish, salmon, squid, scallops, and shrimp. When choosing seafood, make sure it is absolutely fresh. Look for whole fish that have bright eyes, firm flesh, shiny scales, and a fresh sea-like odor. Likewise, choose shellfish that are still tightly locked and closed in their shells, discarding any that are already open.

Fish and seafood can be cooked in various ways, but stir-frying and broiling or grilling are popular methods. In Thailand, whole fish are often steamed, fried, broiled, or baked, skewers of shrimp and scallops are grilled, and fish and seafood are stir-fried or made into curries with subtle yet mouthwatering flavors. Thai fish dishes sometimes include fruit, such as pineapple, papaya, and mango. Many marinades and stir-fry sauces, such as black bean, sweet and sour, or a spicy Szechuan sauce, can be used interchangeably with other fish and seafood, and you may like to adapt the recipes on the following pages to suit your own tastes.

THAI SHRIMP STIR-FRY (PAGE 90)

ORIENTAL ANGLER FISH WITH SWEET & SOUR VEGETABLES

Use a two-layered steamer for this recipe so you can cook the fish in one layer and the vegetables in the other. This fish dish is very low in fat.

SERVES 6

INGREDIENTS:

1½ pounds angler fish tail
6 ounces peeled shrimp, defrosted if
    frozen
4 scallions, chopped
1 red fresh chili, deseeded and
    finely chopped
2 tbsp oyster sauce
6 slices lean Canadian
    bacon

SWEET & SOUR VEGETABLES:

2 zucchini, trimmed
2–3 carrots, peeled
1 red bell pepper, cored and
    deseeded
1½ cups trimmed snow peas
½ tsp grated lemon rind

SAUCE:

1¼ cups fish stock
4 tbsp white wine
    vinegar
1 tbsp superfine sugar
2 tbsp tomato paste
2 tbsp light soy sauce
2 tsp cornstarch, mixed with
    4 tsp cold water

1 ▼ Strip away the skin and membrane from the angler fish. Slice in half by cutting along the sides of the central bone.

2 Lay the fish between 2 layers of parchment paper and flatten to ¼ inch thick with a rolling pin.

3 Mix the remaining ingredients, except the bacon, to form a stuffing.

4 ▼ Press the stuffing onto one half of the fish and top with the other piece. Lay 5 slices of bacon on parchment paper and place the fish on top. Fold the bacon over the fish and cover with the remaining bacon slices. Secure the fish layers with string.

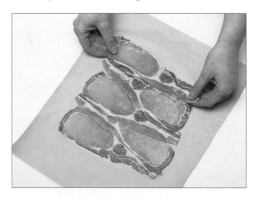

5 Place the fish into 1 compartment of a large steamer. Bring a wok or large pan of water to a boil and put the steamer on top. Cover and steam for 20 minutes.

6 ▲ Meanwhile, slice all the vegetables, except the snow peas. Place in the second steaming compartment with the snow peas and lemon rind. Turn the fish over and place the vegetable compartment on top. Steam for 10 minutes, until cooked.

7 To make sauce, put the ingredients into a pan. Bring to a boil, stirring, and simmer for 5 minutes. Slice the fish and serve with the sweet and sour vegetables and sauce.

BRAISED FISH FILLETS

Any white fish, such as flounder or cod, is ideal for this dish.

SERVES 4

✿✿✿✿✿✿✿✿✿✿✿✿✿✿✿✿✿✿

INGREDIENTS:

3–4 small Chinese dried mushrooms
10–12 ounces white fish fillets
½ egg white, lightly beaten
1 tsp cornstarch paste
(see page 15)
2¼ cups vegetable oil
1 tsp finely chopped fresh ginger
2 scallions, chopped
1 garlic clove, finely chopped
½ small green bell pepper, cored,
deseeded, and cut into small cubes
½ small carrot, thinly sliced
2 ounces canned sliced bamboo shoots,
rinsed and drained
1 tsp salt
½ tsp sugar
1 tbsp light soy sauce
1 tsp Chinese rice wine or dry sherry
1 tbsp chili bean sauce
2–3 tbsp Chinese Stock (see page 10) or
water
few drops of sesame oil
plain boiled rice, to serve

✿✿✿✿✿✿✿✿✿✿✿✿✿✿✿✿✿✿

1 Soak the Chinese mushrooms in warm water for 30 minutes, then drain on paper towels, reserving the soaking water for stock or soup. Squeeze the mushrooms to extract all the moisture, cut off and discard any hard stems, and slice the mushrooms thinly.

2 ▲ Cut the fish fillets into bite-size pieces.

3 Place in a shallow dish and mix with a pinch of salt, the egg white, and cornstarch paste, turning the fish pieces to coat well.

4 ▼ Heat the oil to a temperature of 350–375°F, or until a cube of bread browns in 30 seconds. Deep-fry the fish pieces for about 1 minute. Remove with a slotted spoon and drain on paper towels.

5 Pour off the oil, leaving about 1 tablespoon remaining in the wok.

Add the ginger, scallions, and garlic to flavor the oil for a few seconds. Add the bell pepper, carrot, and bamboo shoots, and stir-fry for about 1 minute.

6 ▼ Add the sugar, soy sauce, rice wine, chili bean sauce, and stock or water. Bring to a boil. Add the fish pieces, stir to coat well with the sauce, and braise for another minute.

7 Sprinkle with sesame oil and serve immediately with rice.

PINEAPPLE & FISH CURRY

This is a fiery hot Thai curry dish, all the better for serving with refreshing (and cooling) pineapple pieces.

SERVES 4

INGREDIENTS:

2 pineapples
3-inch piece galangal, peeled
    and sliced
2 lemon grass stalks, bruised and
    chopped
5 sprigs fresh basil
1 pound firm white fish fillets, such as
    angler fish, halibut, or cod, cubed
4 ounces peeled shrimp
2 tbsp vegetable oil
2 tbsp bottled Thai red curry paste
¼ cup thick coconut milk or cream
2 tbsp Thai fish sauce
2 tsp palm or brown crystal sugar
2–3 fresh red chilies, deseeded and cut
    into thin julienne strips
about 6 kaffir lime leaves, torn
    into pieces
sprigs of cilantro,
    to garnish

1 ▼ Cut the pineapples in half lengthwise. Remove the flesh, reserving the hollowed-out shells for serving if wished. Remove the core from the pineapple flesh, then dice into bite-size pieces.

2 Place the galangal in a large shallow saucepan with the lemon grass and basil. Add the fish cubes and just enough water to cover. Bring to a boil, reduce the heat, and simmer for about 2 minutes.

3 ▼ Add the shrimp to the saucepan and cook for 1 minute more, or until the fish and shrimp are just cooked. Remove the fish and shrimp from the flavored stock with a perforated spoon and keep warm.

4 ▼ Heat the oil in a wok or heavy-based skillet. Add the curry paste and cook for 1 minute. Stir in the coconut milk or cream, fish sauce, brown sugar, chilies, and lime leaves.

5 Add the pineapple and cook until just heated through. Add the cooked fish and mix gently to combine.

6 Spoon into the reserved pineapple shells, if liked, and serve immediately, garnished with cilantro.

SESAME SALMON & CREAM SAUCE

Salmon fillet holds its shape when tossed in sesame seeds and stir-fried. It is served in a creamy turmeric sauce of diced zucchini.

SERVES 4

INGREDIENTS:

1¼–1½ pounds salmon or pink trout
    fillets
2 tbsp light soy sauce
3 tbsp sesame seeds
3 tbsp sunflower oil
4 scallions, thinly sliced
    diagonally
2 large zucchini, diced, or 5-inch
    piece of cucumber, diced
grated rind of ½ lemon
½ tsp turmeric
1 tbsp lemon juice
6 tbsp fish stock or water
3 tbsp heavy cream or
    fromage blanc
salt and pepper
chicory leaves, to garnish
    (optional)

1 ▼ Skin the salmon and cut into strips about 1½ × ¾ inches. Pat dry on paper towels. Season lightly, then brush with soy sauce and sprinkle all over with sesame seeds.

2 Heat 2 tablespoons of oil in the wok, swirling it around until really hot.

3 Add the pieces of salmon and stir-fry for 3–4 minutes, until lightly browned all over. Remove with a fish slice, drain on paper towels, and keep warm.

4 ▼ Add the remaining sunflower oil to the wok. When hot, add the scallions and zucchini or cucumber, and stir-fry for 1–2 minutes. Add the lemon rind and juice, turmeric, stock, and seasoning, and bring the mixture to a boil for a minute or so. Stir the cream or fromage blanc into the sauce.

5 ▲ Return the salmon pieces to the wok and toss gently in the sauce until they are really hot. Serve on warm plates and garnish with chicory leaves, if using.

WRAPPED FISH WITH GINGER BUTTER

This is fish cooked in a healthy, palate-tingling way. Whole mackerel or trout are stuffed with herbs, wrapped in foil, or banana leaves for an even more authentic touch, baked, and then drizzled with a ginger butter.

SERVES 4

INGREDIENTS:
4 × 8-ounce whole trout or mackerel, gutted
4 tbsp chopped fresh cilantro
5 garlic cloves, crushed
2 tsp grated lemon or lime zest
2 tsp vegetable oil
banana leaves, for wrapping (optional)
6 tbsp butter
1 tbsp grated fresh ginger
1 tbsp light soy sauce
salt and pepper

TO GARNISH:
sprigs of fresh cilantro
lemon or lime wedges

1 ▼ Wash and dry the fish. Mix the cilantro with the garlic, lemon or lime zest, and salt and pepper to taste. Spoon into the fish cavities.

2 Brush each fish with a little oil and season well with salt and pepper.

3 ▼ Place each fish on a double thickness of parchment paper or foil and wrap up well to enclose. Alternatively, wrap in banana leaves.

4 ▼ Place on a baking sheet and bake in a preheated oven at 375°F for about 25 minutes, or until the flesh flakes easily.

5 Meanwhile, melt the butter in a small saucepan. Add the grated ginger and stir until well mixed, then stir in the soy sauce.

6 To serve, unwrap the fish packages, drizzle over the ginger butter, and garnish with cilantro and lemon or lime wedges.

FISH IN SZECHUAN HOT SAUCE

This is a classic Szechuan recipe. When served in a restaurant, the fish head and tail are removed before cooking, and you may like to do this.

SERVES 4

INGREDIENTS:
1 carp, porgy, sea bass, trout, grouper, or gray mullet, about 1½ pounds, gutted
1 tbsp light soy sauce
1 tbsp Chinese rice wine or dry sherry
vegetable oil, for deep-frying
sprigs of flat-leaf parsley or cilantro, to garnish

SAUCE:
2 garlic cloves, finely chopped
2–3 scallions, finely chopped
1 tsp finely chopped fresh ginger
2 tbsp chili bean sauce
1 tbsp tomato paste
2 tsp sugar
1 tbsp rice vingar
¼ cup Chinese Stock (see page 10) or water
1 tbsp cornstarch paste (see page 15)
¼ tsp sesame oil

1 ▼ Wash the fish and dry well on paper towels. Score both sides of the fish to the bone with a sharp knife, making diagonal cuts at intervals of about 1 inch. Rub the fish with the soy sauce and rice wine on both sides, then leave on a plate in the refrigerator for 10–15 minutes.

2 Heat the oil in a preheated wok until smoking, to a temperature of 350–375°F. Deep-fry the fish for about 3–4 minutes on both sides, or until golden brown.

3 ▲ Pour off the oil, leaving about 1 tablespoon in the wok. Push the fish to one side of the wok and add the garlic, white parts of the scallions, ginger, chili bean sauce, tomato paste, sugar, vinegar, and Chinese stock or water. Bring to a boil and braise the fish in the sauce for 4–5 minutes, turning it over once.

4 ▼ Add the green parts of the scallions and stir in the cornstarch paste to thicken the sauce. Sprinkle with sesame oil and serve the fish immediately, garnished with fresh parsley or cilantro.

THAI SHRIMP STIR-FRY

A very quick and tasty stir-fry using shrimp and cucumber, cooked with the traditional flavorings of Thai cuisine – lemon grass, chili, and ginger.

SERVES 4

❉❉❉❉❉❉❉❉❉❉❉❉❉❉❉

INGREDIENTS:
1 cucumber
2 tbsp sunflower oil
6 scallions, halved lengthwise and cut
  into 1½-inch lengths
1 lemon grass stalk, thinly sliced
1 garlic clove, chopped
1 tsp chopped fresh red chilli
4 ounces oyster mushrooms
1 tsp chopped fresh ginger
12 ounces cooked, peeled shrimp
2 tsp cornstarch
2 tbsp water
1 tbsp dark soy sauce
¼ tsp Thai fish sauce
2 tbsp Chinese rice wine or
  dry sherry
plain boiled rice,
  to serve

❉❉❉❉❉❉❉❉❉❉❉❉❉❉❉

1 Cut the cucumber into strips, about ¼ × 1½ inches in size.

2 ▼ Heat the sunflower oil in a wok or large heavy-based skillet. Add the scallions, cucumber strips, lemon grass, garlic, chili, oyster mushrooms, and ginger, and stir-fry for about 2 minutes.

3 ▼ Add the shrimp and stir-fry for another minute.

4 In a separate bowl, mix together the cornstarch, water, soy sauce, and fish sauce until smooth.

5 ▼ Stir the cornstarch mixture and rice wine or sherry into the wok or skillet and heat through, stirring, until the sauce has thickened. Serve the shrimp stir-fry immediately, with the boiled rice.

SIZZLED CHILI SHRIMP

*Another Thai classic – large shrimp
marinated in a chili mixture, then
stir-fried with cashews. Serve this
delicious dish with fluffy rice and
braised vegetables.*

SERVES 4

INGREDIENTS:

5 tbsp soy sauce
5 tbsp dry sherry
3 dried red chilies, deseeded and
   chopped
2 garlic cloves, crushed
2 tsp grated fresh ginger
5 tbsp water
1¼ pounds shelled and deveined
   jumbo shrimp
1 large bunch scallions,
   chopped
⅔ cup salted cashews
3 tbsp vegetable oil
2 tsp cornstarch

1 ▼ Mix the soy sauce with the sherry,
chilies, garlic, ginger, and water in a
large bowl.

2 Add the shrimp, scallions, and
cashews, and mix well. Cover tightly
and let marinate for at least 2 hours,
stirring occasionally.

3 ▲ Heat the oil in a wok or large,
heavy-based skillet. Drain the shrimp,
scallions, and cashews from the
marinade with a perforated spoon, and
add them to the wok or skillet,
reserving the marinade. Stir-fry over a
high heat for 1–2 minutes.

4 ▲ Mix the reserved marinade with
the cornstarch, add to the wok or
skillet, and stir-fry for about
30 seconds, until the marinade forms a
slightly thickened shiny glaze over the
shrimp mixture. Serve immediately
with rice.

STIR-FRIED SHRIMP

This colorful and delicious dish is cooked with vegetables: vary them according to seasonal availability.

SERVES 4

❁❁❁❁❁❁❁❁❁❁❁❁❁❁

INGREDIENTS:

¼ cup snow peas
½ small carrot
½ cup baby corn
2 ounces straw mushrooms
6–8 ounces raw jumbo shrimp, peeled
    and deveined
pinch of salt
½ egg white, lightly beaten
1 tsp cornstarch paste
    (see page 15)
about 1¼ cups vegetable oil
1 scallion, trimmed and cut into
    short pieces
4 slices fresh ginger, peeled and finely
    chopped
½ tsp sugar
1 tbsp light soy sauce
1 tsp Chinese rice wine or
    dry sherry
few drops of sesame oil

❁❁❁❁❁❁❁❁❁❁❁❁❁❁

1 Trim the snow peas. Scrub the carrot and thinly cut it in pieces, about the same size as the snow peas. Cut the baby corn and straw mushrooms in half.

2 ▲ In a bowl, mix the shrimp with a pinch of salt, the egg white, and cornstarch paste.

3 ▼ Heat a wok over a high heat for 2–3 minutes, then add the oil and heat to medium-hot before adding the shrimp; stir to separate them. Remove with a perforated spoon as soon as the color changes.

4 ▼ Pour off the oil, leaving about 1 tablespoon in the wok. Add all the vegetables and stir-fry for about 1 minute. Add the shrimp and the seasonings. Blend well. Sprinkle with sesame oil and serve hot.

SZECHUAN SHRIMP

Raw shrimp should be used if possible; otherwise, omit steps 1 and 2, and add the ready-cooked shrimp before the sauce ingredients at the beginning of step 3.

SERVES 4

INGREDIENTS:
8–10 ounces raw jumbo shrimp
pinch of salt
½ egg white, lightly beaten
1 tsp cornstarch paste
    (see page 15)
2½ cups vegetable oil
fresh cilantro leaves,
    to garnish

SAUCE:
1 tsp finely chopped fresh
    ginger
2 scallions, finely chopped
1 garlic clove, finely chopped
3–4 small dried red chilies, deseeded
    and chopped
1 tbsp light soy sauce
1 tsp Chinese rice wine or
    dry sherry
1 tbsp tomato paste
1 tbsp oyster sauce
2–3 tbsp Chinese Stock (see page 10)
    or water
few drops of sesame oil

1 ▲ Peel the raw shrimp, then mix with the salt, egg white, and cornstarch paste until well coated.

2 ▼ Heat the oil in a preheated wok until it is smoking, at a temperature of 350–375°F. Deep-fry the shrimp in the hot oil for about 1 minute. Remove with a perforated spoon and drain on paper towels.

3 Pour off the oil, leaving about 1 tablespoon in the wok.

4 ▼ Add all the ingredients for the sauce to the wok, bring the sauce mixture to a boil, and stir until smooth and well blended.

5 Add the deep-fried shrimp to the Szechuan sauce and stir until well blended. Serve garnished with fresh cilantro leaves.

FRIED SQUID FLOWERS

The addition of green bell pepper and black bean sauce to the squid makes a colorful and delicious dish.

SERVES 4

INGREDIENTS:
12–14 ounces prepared and cleaned squid (see page 38)
1 medium green bell pepper, cored and deseeded
3–4 tbsp vegetable oil
1 garlic clove, finely chopped
¼ tsp finely chopped fresh ginger
2 tsp finely chopped scallions
¼ tsp salt
2 tbsp crushed black bean sauce
1 tsp Chinese rice wine or dry sherry
few drops of sesame oil

1 ▲ Open up the squid and score in a crisscross pattern. Cut the squid into small pieces.

2 ▲ Blanch in a bowl of boiling water for a few seconds. Remove and drain; dry well on paper towels.

3 ▲ Cut the bell pepper into small triangular pieces. Heat the oil in a preheated wok, or a heavy-based skillet, and stir-fry the bell pepper for about 1 minute. Add the garlic, ginger, scallion, salt, and squid. Continue stirring for another minute.

4 ▲ Finally, add the black bean sauce and rice wine or sherry, and blend well. Serve hot, sprinkled with drops of sesame oil.

SPICED SCALLOPS

Scallops are available both fresh and frozen. Make sure they are completely defrosted before cooking.

SERVES 4

INGREDIENTS:

12 large scallops with roe attached, defrosted if frozen, or 12 ounces small scallops without roe, defrosted if frozen
4 tbsp sunflower oil
4–6 scallions, thinly sliced diagonally
1 garlic clove, crushed
1-inch piece fresh ginger, finely chopped
2 cups trimmed snow peas
1¼ cups sliced button or closed-cup mushrooms
2 tbsp sherry
2 tbsp soy sauce
1 tbsp liquid honey
¼ tsp ground allspice
salt and pepper
1 tbsp sesame seeds, toasted

1 Wash and dry the scallops, discarding any black pieces. Detach the roe, if using them. Slice each scallop into 3–4 pieces. If the roes are large, halve them.

2 ▲ Heat 2 tablespoons of sunflower oil in a wok, swirling it around until really hot. Add the scallions, garlic, and ginger, and stir-fry for a minute or so, then add the snow peas and

continue to cook for 2–3 minutes, stirring continuously. Transfer the mixture to a bowl.

3 ▼ Add the remaining oil to the wok. When it is really hot, add the scallops and roe and stir-fry for a couple of minutes. Add the mushrooms and continue to cook for another minute or so.

4 ▼ Add the sherry, soy sauce, honey, and allspice to the wok, with salt and pepper to taste. Mix thoroughly, then return the snow pea mixture to the wok.

5 Season well and toss together over a high heat for a minute or so, until piping hot. Serve immediately, sprinkled with sesame seeds.

INDEX